CW01496512

Flying In Faith – Letters Home

– LAURA WESTLEY –

An environmentally friendly book printed and bound in England by
www.printondemand-worldwide.com

Mixed Sources
Product group from well-managed
forests, and other controlled sources
www.fsc.org Cert no. TT-COC-002641
© 1996 Forest Stewardship Council

PEFC Certified

This product is
from sustainably
managed forests
and controlled
sources

www.pefc.org

PEFC/16-33-415

www.fast-print.net/store.php

Flying In Faith – Letters Home
Copyright © Flying in Faith 2012

ISBN 978-178035-253-4

First published 2012 by
FASTPRINT PUBLISHING
Peterborough, England.

Dedication

Dedicated to:

My wonderful husband, Mike, for being strong enough to be different; Deborah and Ivan for the joy they have brought into our lives; my mom, for teaching me to believe in myself; our MAF supporters, for their love and faithfulness;and to God, for lovingly working it all out for His glory.

Contents

Introduction.

We left knowing we would learn more than teach, receive more than give, and grow within ourselves. They have to have been four of the most interesting years of my life! We 'wrote home' to our friends and supporters quite simply because we knew that they loved us and held us aloft in prayer, and because we loved them for their care and their faithfulness.

There is only so much you can write in newsletters. They show only a part of our lives with MAF. A thousand things happened about which we have never written. Over the years Mike and I just knew that 'that' amazing encounter with so-and-so, or the close shave with a demented taxi-driver, or the snakes that never got near us, were all God honouring the prayers of our faithful supporters. We are forever meeting people in Church who have supported MAF for 1, 2, 20, 30, or 40 years! MAF has been operating successfully since just after World War II; what a witness to their faithfulness!

If you are thinking of going out to the mission field, whether in your street, town, or on another continent, may we encourage you to treasure your supporters?

Their love is something quite special; unique, uplifting and empowering.

If you support someone on the mission field, thank you! Please know that it is impossible to work on the mission field without your prayers and support. We knew we were prayed for and that gave us great strength through our dark times and it helped us to keep focused during all the other times. Know, too, that God values highly your prayers and that what you offer up is a fragrant sacrifice to the Lord.

With our love,

Mike and Laura.

News from Mike and Laura: June 2005

Wow, what an exciting last few months! We are thrilled to share with you what you, as Mission Aviation Fellowship (MAF) supporters, are part of. MAF is a charity that reaches all over the globe and you, with us, are part of this amazing family and what God achieves through it.

We have spent the last 2 months at the MAF US headquarters in Redlands, California, where we both successfully completed the MAF Flight Orientation Course. It was tough! We flew over mountains, through deep valleys, in the desert, in blistering dust and heat, through fog and rain, all the while learning to find and then land on steep airstrips that looked more like badly maintained postage stamps. At times it was very tough and we knew, deep down inside, that we were not alone. We gained much encouragement from knowing that you were encouraging and praying for us and that God was listening. We knew He was with you as He was with us. We praise and thank Him for you and for the many hours of safe flying that we all completed, as well as the successful completion of this pass-or-fail course. Note

the 'family' photo below - we are from all over the world
and going to many different places!

<u>Redlands Class of May 2005</u>

From top Left to Right:
Trevor of MAF Canada; off to Asia
Dwight of MAF US; off to Mozambique
Mike and Laura MAF UK; off to Uganda
Paul; Chief Flying Instructor
Brian; Instructor
Larry; Instructor
Martin of MAF Switzerland; off to Tanzania
Kees of MAF US; off to Papua
Kent; Instructor
Dave; Instructor

Our instructors had all flown in various MAF
programmes around the world and their heart was to pass
on as much wisdom as they could about *all* aspects of

missionary flying. Many of these people have served with MAF for over 15 years and we were blessed to be mentored and trained by them. Praise God for godly instructors who go the extra mile!

There is a very busy MAF maintenance hangar in Redlands as well; they are preparing two Amphibious Caravan aircraft for Indonesia where MAF's post-tsunami relief work continues. We met some of the folk who had worked in Indonesia, helping out with the tsunami relief, and we heard from them how they too were encouraged by the prayers of others.

In the Redlands Hangar

We are due to arrive in Uganda mid-September so we shall be spending the next few weeks telling churches about the work of MAF. We also need to decide what to pack - water filters, mosquito nets, malaria tablets and the like. We need to find a big suitcase!

We ask that you pray for us during this time of transition. We are excited, yet will need to learn an awful lot in a very short time. We will have challenging weather to contend with, will need to fly into some areas of political unrest, and will be under the constant evaluation of the Chief Pilot in Uganda for the first 6 months. We will also need to adapt to the new culture, so we need God's wisdom in abundance. We also need to say our 'goodbyes' to friends and family. One of my parents unexpectedly passed away whilst I was in Redlands and I was not able to be there for the funeral or for my family. Please pray for our families too, as they sacrifice something as well when we leave for Uganda.

We praise and thank God for His goodness, love & faithfulness! We testify to His work in the lives of many whom you help MAF to reach. We thank you all for your love and prayers. Please let us know if you would like us to pray for you or others you know. Have a super summer.

"You fill me with joy in your presence." Psalm 16:11

On 1 June my stepmother passed away very unexpectedly of ovarian cancer. No one knew she was ill, or even suspected that she had cancer. My dad, struggling to come to grips with such a sudden loss, never managed to contact me, and one of my brothers sent me an email. So I learnt of her death in an email; this was hard. Even harder was discovering that there was no way I could get from the USA to South Africa in time for her funeral.

Exactly 30 days later, Mike's dad was tragically killed in a motorbike crash in Essex, UK. Mike and his family were totally devastated. We spent most of July and August coming to terms with this loss, with attending funerals and memorial services, etc. It was surreal, knowing that we were about to go to Uganda in a few weeks time and each very unexpectedly losing a parent.

Lord, you have held us so tightly! Thank you for your faithfulness. We have achieved the seemingly impossible and succeeded at Redlands; Your Word is so true: what is impossible for man is possible with God!

My heart hurts to know that I wasn't there for Mmum's funeral and that I never got to say goodbye. So sudden, yet You always knew it would be this way. Please fill me with your peace over this situation.

I pray, too, for Mike. His whole being is mourning and he is deeply distressed. I hardly know what to say or what to do to help him over this. Please hold him close, please comfort him.

Thank you for all those who are praying for us; somehow that reassures me and builds me up. Please bless them!

In Jesus' name I pray, Amen.

News from Mike and Laura: 25 September 2005

To our dearest MAF Family.

"First, I thank my God through Jesus Christ for all of you, because your faith is being reported all over the world."

Romans 1 vs8.

The aircraft descended cautiously through the storm clouds, tracing a predetermined yet invisible path through the sky that would safely get us onto the tarmac at an airport where there was no radar to guide us in. So it was that our first glimpses of Uganda were small patches of deep green that poked up through the swirling masses of grey clouds as we descended over Entebbe airport. And then, quite suddenly, we were on the runway peering out at lush green grass and trees and a slate-grey Lake Victoria. We taxied up to the terminal building, passing several Russian transport aircraft, some with 'UN' painted on the side. The smell of fresh rain, the humidity and heat, together with 'mosquito squadron 1', bombarded us as we climbed down the aircraft stairs. Mike and I joined the immigration queue where Gerrit Pap, MAF Uganda's Chief Pilot, met us. We used our 50 minutes there to get to know each other! Two out of 3 suitcases made it to Entebbe, so we got to know the lost baggage lady quite well too. 1 bag had gone missing somewhere in South Africa and would turn up 10 days later courtesy of Richard Owen, Bundy's Bible (Mike's late dad) being inside it. One-and-a-half hours after we arrived, we left the terminal. The clouds had turned a very dark grey and the temperature dropped several degrees as we walked to our van. At 1545hrs the sky opened. Torrential rain turned the red sand roads into muddy by-ways as we drove past a cacophony of huts, houses, goats and cows, and banana and papaya trees. *Bodaboda* (bike) drivers jostled with *matatu* (10-seat taxi) drivers and *muzungus* (foreigners like us) for a place on the road. Quite suddenly we all came to a halt - the thunderstorm had brought down a tree. 2 lanes of traffic turned into 6, 4 in our direction and 2 in the other, as everyone tried to get past the leafy obstruction. Within minutes we had armed soldiers passing by our window, making sure no one got too out of hand. Someone produced a saw which, in turn, produced a queue for free firewood. Just before 1800hrs we reached the home of Pam and Stan Lincoln, who were kindly housing us for the first several days. It was already dark. At 1805hrs the electricity in Kampala was turned off. We had arrived in equatorial Africa...

Our heartfelt thanks to all of you for your prayers and support. As we shared in our first newsletter, my stepmother passed away on 1 June. On 1 July Mike's father was killed in a motorbike accident in the UK. We spent 3 weeks in the UK sorting our paperwork and the funeral near Salisbury. We managed to let many of you know, and the prayers you offered have been answered as we can testify to the Lord's goodness, faithfulness and strength during this time. Mike and I decided to fly to South Africa on 20 July to be with our families. Mike's family had a memorial service for his dad in Port Elizabeth and we spent 3 weeks with his mum there, supporting and encouraging each other. Mike's parents' church was wonderful, as were the churches of his aunts and uncles. We spent a week with my father in Johannesburg; he had been grieving alone for 7 weeks and then 2 weeks with my mum, step-dad and brothers and their families in Cape Town. We also visited Mark, who works as an Ambassador for Sport missionary in Polsmoor prison, Cape Town. That man is a light in a dark place! Many young men in the prison are coming to know Christ through his work there! We were constantly in the Lord's care and had many opportunities to share our faith and the reason for our hope. We know that the Lord is in control of all things all of the time. We are also both so aware that, often, it was just knowing that so many people were praying for us that got us through.

Apart from medical evacuation flights and charter flights for missions, relief and development agencies, churches and NGOs, MAF Uganda has several 'regular' flight schedules. On Mondays, Wednesdays and Fridays we fly to Gulu, Kitgum and Kalongo. On Tuesdays, Thursdays and Fridays we fly to Amudat, Matany, Moroto, Kotido, Kaabong and Southern Sudan. For example, MAF flights support the work of GOAL in Kalongo. GOAL provides medical and public health programmes. We also fly to Bundibugyo to support the work of World Harvest Mission there. It is wonderful to see just how many people there are working for so many different agencies, all with the common goal of spreading the love of Christ and the message of salvation in whatever way God has called them to. And all over the world it is people like you who make it possible for people like Mike and I to be here. **Your role is vital.**

Please pray for:

❖ Mark, working in Polsmoor prison. He is praying for someone to work alongside him. He and his wife are expecting their first child this week.

❖ MAF representatives Andy and Angela, Jim and Anne, and Andrew and Marilynn.

❖ Izzy, for wisdom and continued vision as she continues leading the Bible-study programme at Sunnyhill Church.

❖ The work of Hannah House in Westcliffe, Bournemouth.

❖ Andy Mortimore on board the *Logos II* with OM.

❖ Raewyn, Peter and Rayne, as they seek new housing.

❖ Keith and Leanne, as they prepare for marriage in April 2006.

❖ Us, as we study for our Ugandan Commercial Pilot Licences and start the final stage of our MAF flying training programme. Please pray that we will resist the temptation to try doing things in our strength and our timing and, rather, trusting God for His strength and His timing. Pray that we settle in to the Ugandan culture and that God keeps us humble enough to learn from these wonderful people, instead of trying to do things 'our' way.

Please let us know if we can pray for you, your church, etc. in any specific way.

Mukama abwe oma kisa! (God bless you!) With our love and thanks, Mike and Laura.

Lord, where to start?! It is good to know that You are in control of all of this! You have placed us here and we are glad to be here. Everything is so different; it sounds, feels, smells and breathes 'different'. It's fantastic and a little scary. You have placed us within a great team and I thank you for that. We have much to sort out and plan - work permits, Customs, CAA exams, medicals and the rest, so I commit all these things to You. Grant us favour and guide us. In Jesus' name I pray, Amen.

News from Mike and Laura: 25 November 2005

To our dearest MAF Family

1 Thessalonians 1v2-3&3v9 "We always thank God for all of you, mentioning you in our prayers. We continually remember before our God and Father your work produced by faith, your labour prompted by love, and your endurance inspired by hope in our Lord Jesus Christ. How can we thank God enough for you in return for all the joy we have in the presence of God because of you?"

Clutching the huge steering-wheel of work's old Land Rover, sweat pouring off our arms in the 35°C heat, I navigated the old beast past muddy potholes and through the swarms of taxis, motorbikes and crowds of people along the Entebbe to Kampala road. That day, driving home from the airport was a significant day for us as we had both finally passed our MAF Uganda training. Mike had done his first post-training flight for MAF a few days before, and I had just finished with my very first flight. It had been a year, almost to the day, since we had applied to MAF Europe and we look back and see God's hand in it all and praise and thank Him for the privilege of being here. Parts of Kampala were ablaze as political unrest erupted, yet our trip home remained safe and I was reminded of Romans 16 verse 20: "The God of peace will soon crush Satan under your feet."

We want to share with you all a little of what **you** are making possible here in Uganda and Sudan. Two of the really fantastic things about this 'job' are the people we get to meet and the things we get to be part of. Here are a few examples.

Mike did his training in Dar Es Salem, Tanzania, in mid-October. He was there for 10 days and, during that time, not only did God provide him with the strength and wisdom to get through his training, but He also kept Mike safe through the political unrest there at the time. God also provided in a more unusual way on the day when the aircraft's nosewheel got a bit stuck in the mud at a remote airstrip. The place was infested with lions, which made walking anywhere impossible unless you wanted to become lion lunch! As it happened, God promptly sent help by way of a Boeing 767 pilot, who was on holiday driving about in his car. He provided the extra muscle-power needed to dislodge the aircraft. God in the detail! Each prayer you offered up answered.

Mike & British church planters to Fort Portal

During my training we 'medevaced' a young Ugandan man in Northern Uganda who had been shot through the neck. Without your prayers and support he would have never been safely reached, or have never been afforded the opportunity to be flown out to a hospital where he could receive medical treatment. Driving was not an option, as the Lord's Resistance Army (LRA) is active in these areas. That's how he ended up with the wound in the first place. We flew him to Kalongo Catholic Mission Hospital, where they ministered to him. Please pray for his continued healing in body and spirit.

Laura back from Pader

One day Mike landed at Matany, an airstrip out in the middle of a large expanse of wilderness. As they taxied in they could see a huge cloud of dust approaching. A small, white speck soon appeared ahead of it, which later transformed itself into a white 4x4. Moments later, following a deftly executed handbrake turn, it screeched to a halt alongside the aircraft. Picture Mike's face, if you will, when a tiny, 65-year-old nun stepped out of it to pick up the passenger! Buckets of love and enthusiasm flowed from her as she greeted Mike and welcomed him to Uganda and expressed how thankful she was for the service MAF provided. Time and time again people tell us that MAF is the only safe way in and out of their particular area.

Let me tell you about Anne, a German Child Social Worker who was out in Uganda for a couple of weeks.

MAF flew her up to Morulem, where she assisted several local children's charities. Anne stayed with us for 4 nights, telling us of the nights she slept on the floor to stay well out of harm's way at night when all the shooting was going on, of the horrors she saw inflicted upon the children, of the folk working up there to show Love - the other way. She left us a note, part of which I share with you as it involves you all: "I also want to encourage you to keep on working with MAF. People in the North depend on this connection with the world outside their community so much, due to the lack of transport and security. And if it is only hope you bring with the landing aircraft: that there is life outside and that somebody cares - it is vital for people. If you could only see the smile in the faces of the people telling you that things will improve now because the airstrip is there. And even the week gets a new face because thrice the aircraft may possibly land." We want you to know what it is you, by God's grace, make possible. None of this is possible without you.

We also met Wayne and Beverly from Australia. This retired couple is setting up a charity, Cornerstone Foundation (Australia) Inc., that helps orphaned teenagers in the Kitgum area. The charity provides education and skills training to youngsters so that these war-scarred young people can earn a living, regain their self-respect and dignity, and learn about Christ. We were so blessed to fly them there and back, to be a support to them and to allow them to share their vision with us as they ministered to us, infecting us with their hope and enthusiasm. They have given us permission to release their photo and email address:

wbstevenscfa@ozemail.com.au

Wayne and Beverly, Cornerstone Foundation

Christmas is approaching and we think of all the various people we know all over the world and of how different the various celebrations will be. Yet we also know that for all of us there will be the one common thing: Christ, the Prince of Peace. We want to wish you all a wonderful Christmas season. We pray that God bless you in every way possible. We pray that you, your families and friends, have a safe, happy and blessed time together. As we reflect on the Prince of Peace, we ask that you join us praying for:

- Wayne and Beverly of Cornerstone Foundations.

- Leanne and Keith, getting married in April.

- The work of Hannah House, Westcliffe, Bournemouth.

- Chris, Megan and their new baby!

- Peace in Uganda and Sudan.

- Safety for us all here as we work and fly in these troubled areas.

- Praise and thanks for our safe and successful training and God's constant love and care.

God bless, love Mike and Laura.

Lord, the impact of MAF, its real impact, is way more amazing than I realised. You have birthed and grown and protected this fellowship and I am amazed to see what You are doing through her. I am seeing depravation on a new level, fear in people as I have never had to experience it, an incredible suffering of hundreds of thousands of people at the hands of a few. So much is hostile; the weather, the roads, the madmen with guns, riots and political unrest. Lord, thank you for keeping us safe. Just driving home in one piece is a miracle! You are in control and that is just so good to know! Thank you for those who pray for us; will they ever know just how important it is? Lord, let them know, let them understand the depth and need of their prayers in this battle. In Jesus' name, Amen.

Charter to Mbarara: 15 January 2006

On Saturday 14 January I was privileged to fly 3 CBM (Christian Blind Mission) managers (2 Americans based in Nairobi and one Dutchman based in Kampala) from Kajjansi to Mbarara. Leaving behind a dusty and busy Capital, we headed out towards the far south-west of Uganda. White and grey skies stood in sharp contrast to the lush green hills and deep blue lakes we flew past. An hour later we were approaching Mbarara, a small town to the east of the Rwenzori Mountains. The one-hour flight in our Cessna 206 had just saved the passengers from a 16-hour drive.

The CBM team had come to visit the Ruharo Mission Hospital and Eye Clinic. This modest complex provides orthopaedic and ophthalmic services to the local community. Around 1,300 eye operations and around 700 other operations are carried out annually! The hospital also has a special outreach to disabled children. Dr Kenneth Kagame, the eye hospital's Director, took our group around, explaining the changes they had made in the last year, where things had been better organised, new needs noted and acted upon, buildings extended - all to improve the services offered. He then shared the hospital's plans and hopes for the future, what was needed, what they hoped to improve on.

It was in the eye ward that I first met Dr Tindyebwa Lubovica. She was examining an old lady's eyes. A long queue of people, all ages, waited patiently in the corridor to see her. Later that day we sat down and got talking. Her story inspires me.

Dr Lubovica was born near Mbarara. Her father, an orphan, was raised by Catholic priests at a nearby mission. He went on to train as a teacher. Her mother was a full-time housewife. She managed the family's land, digging, planting and sowing the food. Together the couple raised 10 children, 8 of whom went to university and 2 to college. Dr Lubovica shared about her childhood. She told me how their life had been simple in the village, how all the money earned from the crops had been saved to send them to school, how their joint suffering through hard times had brought them together and forged strong bonds of family love. Dr Lubovica worked hard at school and spent her holidays working the land, helping the family to 'move on'. Her motivation to do well at school was a hug and a big "thank you" from dad. Dr Lubovica won a scholarship from the Ugandan government to go and train as a doctor at Makere University in Kampala. She graduated in 1991 and spent the next 4 years working in Casualty at Mulago Hospital, Kampala. She went back to Makere University to specialise in Ophthalmology and, in 1999, went to Arua, working in the hospital there. Her husband and daughter were the only survivors of a group ambushed by the LRA. As a result of this traumatic experience the family decided to move out of the area and went to Mbale, where she worked in the regional hospital for two-and-a-half years. Over the years Dr Lubovica had provided 'relief cover' for various eye doctors that worked for CBM, as they went to meetings, training courses, etc., and last year she was asked by CBM to join them at Mbarara.

Dr Lubovica shares that the biggest motivator for her to join CBM was the opportunity to work in a hospital that had proper equipment, where the equipment worked, and where the staff worked and were well-motivated. Her second motivation was a good salary, which she now uses to put not only her own 2 children through school but also several of her nieces and nephews. Her third motivation was that Mbarara is 'near home' and that, to be able to be with her mother, now 78, was a blessing she is thankful for.

Dr Lubovica went on to share much more about 'family'. "As you grow up the hard times you go through together makes you friends. If later you become successful you pay to keep the others in your family. This suffering together helps keep the friendship and this helping each other helps preserve the security and strength of the family. We normally only get together as a family to bury someone but recently my siblings and I decided to have a feast. So we got a cow and some goat, hired transport and invited all our family. Over 1,000 (!) people from our family attended and we had a great time of feasting and laughing. Some of us had not seen each other for 10 years."

We talked about HIV/AIDS, how entire families had been wiped out and "the doors to their homes closed forever." We talked about the food Uganda has, her fertile soils being able to produce something to eat in around 3 months. She explained to me that people sow millet and cassava for the dry season (August to December) and so people could survive easily where there is peace. She hoped for peace for the people in the north.

We talked about politics, how colonialism had exploited Uganda but at the same time brought progress, her hopes and fears for the upcoming general election. She said: "People know what they want in terms of self-development".

Dr Lubovica spoke to me about the NGOs. She explained how at least 70% of all the NGO money went on NGO cars, on sustaining expensive NGO family lifestyles. "Whites bring the money in but they take it back out with them." She shared about pay differences; how an expatriate earned several times more than the Ugandan they were working alongside did, doing the same job and with the same training.

I asked the doctor what she needed in her hospital and she explained that they really need a 'tonopen', a tonometer. This measures pressure on the eye and is really needed for work with children. A second-hand one costs around £1,500.

I flew the CBM team out at 3pm that day. They will be flying to various other hospitals in Uganda this coming week. When we arrived back at Kajjansi I asked them what their main objective had been. They shared that it was to build upon the local partnership. "This is the real basis for the work done. Our heart is to build relationships and so help disabled men, women and children."

I came home knowing a little more about Uganda. I was given a glimpse into the heart of one Ugandan lady who, just like me, has ideas, opinions, hopes and dreams for the future. I thought again of how Christ came to restore sight to the blind, not only those in body but those blind in spirit.

"But you are a chosen people, a royal priesthood, a holy nation, a people belonging to God, **SO THAT** you may declare the praises of him who called you out of darkness and into his wonderful light." 1 Peter 2v9.

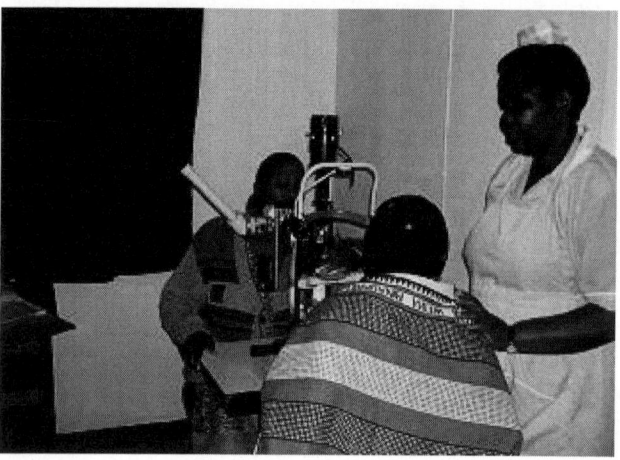

Dr Lubovica at work

Mike and Dr Lubovica

CBM boarding

Lord, I am very challenged by what I learnt today. I am humbled to meet someone who is so unselfish, so passionate, so dedicated to not only her family but to her work and her country. I have learnt a lot today; about Uganda, about life here, and about You. As I consider my selfishness, please show me the areas where I am selfish and need to change and guide me towards unselfishness. I know that there are many and it will take some time, but I trust You to do it gently. In Jesus' name, Amen.

News from Mike and Laura: 14 February 2006

December 2005

Last night we had a huge, full moon. Just before 7pm she started her regal ascent over the city of Kampala, dressed in a bright red-orange. The dry season has arrived! With it, red dust and immense heat. The dust stubbornly hangs in the air day and night, leading to the most glorious of sunsets and the red moon-rise. It covers everything else. Our feet leave little red patches on the tiles; our books, clothes, photos and everything else carry a fine film of red. The grass is slowly going brown and drying up, plants take on a wilted look and start their slow march towards semi-death. Creation here has started to hold her breath, bracing herself for the next 3 months of drought and heat. In Northern Uganda, immense bush fires are started to burn the grasslands and encourage new growth. As we fly above it we see vast tracts of blackened land accompanied by plumes of black smoke that wraps itself around small mountains and weaves itself between storm clouds that bear no rain. We all start to walk slower. Even the birds seem to fly slower. Our garden has a small, coniferous tree in it which Mike has decorated with tinsel and baubles. The bright bands and balls of gold and red flash in the sunlight, providing a somewhat surreal contrast to the passing political broadcasts blaring out from car-mounted loudspeakers in an unfamiliar language. Posters of President Museveni and other presidential contenders have started to appear on walls and windows, telephone poles and taxis. Young people all over Uganda await the results of exams just written, painfully aware of the financial and personal cost of failure. Folk at church praise God for providing the 3,000 Shillings (£1) they needed for that day's meal, whilst others pray for the money needed to send their child to school, to pay for malaria medicine, for God to heal their AIDS. Our lives exist in such deep contrast. We are exceptionally well-off by comparison. Yet, for the many material needs we see, we also see a joy and contentment here that we have not seen in Europe. Children skip down the road singing, they wave enthusiastically as they greet you with a big smile. They get to play outside in big, loud, noisy groups. Ladies sing softly or chat away happily to their friends as they hand-wash the family's clothes in a plastic tub outside. It is not uncommon to see someone doing an impromptu dance as he or she waits for the *mutatu* (mini-bus) to arrive. Not many people here worry about pension plans or how their investments are doing. Today is lived for today. So it is here, in this new environment, that Mike and I find ourselves. Here to learn as we fly. At times we struggle to cope with what we see. At times we are humbled by others' faith that lives by the day, their faith so strengthened by its everyday application to survival. At the moment we are struggling to learn how to do without privacy, without time off and *with* using a computer. This seems quite pathetic in contrast! But we know that He is here, with us always, guiding us as we go. Teaching us, growing us and stretching us.

Talking of stretching... The lady who works in flight bookings had the week before Christmas off. This meant that Mike was required to spend the week in 'Ops' (Operations) doing her job. He says he was stretched! With what he describes as 'meltdown' he and Steve spent the week dashing about trying to contend with pilots being ill, an aircraft being in maintenance longer than expected, loads of people wanting to fly and "had their booking been done, and if not why not?" - and all this to the strains of '*Silent Night... all is calm... all is bright*'!!! There is a lot more to MAF than flying.

The New Year means we all get to count every nut, bolt and other bit in the hangar.

We are part of a team that includes engineers, flight followers, accountants, vehicle mechanics, logistics personnel, security guards and various other airfield staff. We have people from all over the world; the Congo, Uganda, Kenya, the US and Europe. And then there is you, a vital part of the team, the hidden backbone.

Christmas Day

The church is decorated with lots of brightly-coloured balloons and pink bows that somehow hide the rusting tin roof and highlight the 'birthday' aspect of the day. A forlorn-looking fir tree stands in the corner, thirsty, dressed in balloons and lights. I am dressed in new trousers from mum-in-law, creased (straight out of the wrapping), and Mike is all in khaki, looking like a lost Game Ranger. "The rhinoceros is over theeere..." he quips. Everyone else is dressed in their finest. Evening dresses, suits and grand party dresses. Children's fancy shoes and white socks, beaded hair and bows. Even small boys are tottering around in 3-piece suits! The warden asks all visitors to make themselves known by a "show of arms". We half expect a metallic rustle as a rash of AK-47s is raised, but no, it is a show of hands he is after. Mike and I exchange a smile. I am sitting on the pew, gazing out of the window as folk go up front with their offerings. Beyond the barred, dust-drenched arch window I see a sun-bleached, pale-blue sky, a browning palm tree, thorn trees and vast areas of red earth. We stand to sing 'Silent Night' and the balloons start to pop with the heat, piercing our angelic singing with loud bangs. We all file up front to take communion from the Archbishop, whose robes are the only reminder of England amidst the heat and dust and hubbub of Africa.

"He will be great and will be called the Son of the Most High. The Lord God will give him the throne of David and he will reign over the house of Jacob forever; his kingdom will never end."
Luke 1: 32-33

Friday, 30 December, 12 noon.

We have just returned from buying milk and eggs from the 'shops' at the top of our road. It has been an education! There is a huge gathering of soldiers, policemen, political activists and citizens. The music is blaring away, dancers are dancing and hundreds of whistles are blowing, sending shrill stabs of sound into the vast cacophony of noise. We have a camera with us and so are told that we can not go into the rally unless we take our camera home. We join a group of people standing at the edge of the 'park' where the rally is being held, and we are all moved on by the soldiers. As the only *muzungus* about, we manage to draw the scowls and stares of every soldier and policeman! The normally bustling market has turned into a huge, swollen, steaming mass of bodies. Yellow hats and whistles are being sold, posters given away. Hundreds of *mutatus* (taxis) driving into and out of the area simultaneously send clouds of dust into the air whilst providing a live-or-die exercise in crossing the road. A band is trumpeting and drumming away, each member dressed-up in bright red tunics and black trousers, sweating it out under the noonday sun. A Russian Mil-8 helicopter passes overhead. A plain-clothes policeman asks us to move on and go home...

Children in remote Southern Sudan

Mike and I have been doing quite a lot of flying. On Saturday 14 January I was privileged to fly 3 Christian Blind Mission managers (CBM) and my off-duty husband from Kajjansi to Mbarara. Leaving behind a dusty and busy Capital, we headed out towards the far south-west of Uganda. White and grey skies stood in sharp contrast to the lush green hills and deep blue lakes we flew past. An hour later we were approaching Mbarara, a small town to the east of the Rwenzori Mountains. The one-hour flight in our Cessna 206 had just saved the passengers from a 16-hour drive.

The CBM team had come to visit the Ruharo Mission Hospital and Eye Clinic. This modest complex provides orthopaedic and ophthalmic services to the local community. Around 1,300 eye operations and around 700 other operations are carried out annually! The hospital also has a special outreach to disabled children. Dr Kenneth Kagame, the eye hospital's Director, took our group around, explaining the changes they had made in the last year, where things had been better organised, new needs noted and acted upon, buildings extended- all to improve the services offered. He then shared the hospital's plans and hopes for the future, what was needed, what they hoped to improve on. This complex is one of 3 in Uganda that CBM works with. There is another hospital in Kampala and the third hospital lies to the far east of Uganda, in Tororo. Each of these hospitals carries out roughly 1000 cataract operations a year and around 1,000 orthopaedic operations. MAF was able to fly the CBM managers to the 3 locations in 3 days, so helping them achieve a lot in a short time. CBM's heart is to build strong relationships with the local people working in these hospitals so that many more disabled (blind, visually impaired, etc.) people can be helped. They do this by helping them to identify needs where eyesight and other disabilities are a consideration, and fund various programmes within their community. This includes education in schools (for both teachers and pupils) and health-related precautions that can be taken.

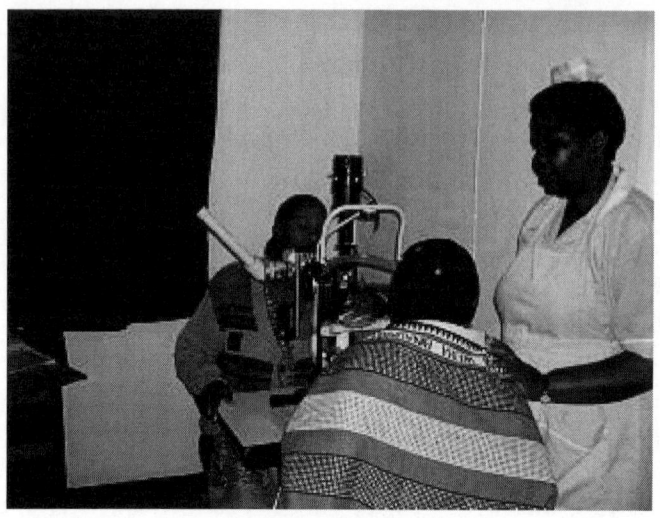

Dr Lubovica working at the Ruharo Eye Hospital,
Mbarara

*"Whether he is a sinner or not, I don't know. One thing I know.
I was blind but now I see." John 9: 25*

Last week I flew into Lokutok, Sudan, with 2 ministers
from the Bible Institute. It was the first MAF aircraft to
land there and we were given a really warm welcome and
that not only because it was 40°C on the day! I met Steve
and Iris and their 4 young children. They have been in
Lokutok since December. This missionary family really
inspired me. Their heart is to introduce the local people
here to the Gospel and to train and build-up local
pastors. 8 people have been killed here in the last month,
mostly due to tribal revenge. There was an LRA ambush
on their compound last year. They are living in a run-
down house with no electricity, no toilets, etc., in the
incredible heat and dust and amidst much insecurity.
And yet their love of the Lord just filled their home.

They do not get to see many other people from 'the outside' and it brought home to me how much of a lifeline to many missionary families MAF really is. So your support of MAF not only affects us and the work we do, but it reaches and affects the lives of many other missionaries as well. It supports them in their various fields and encourages them in whatever endeavour God has called them to.

One of MAF South Africa's Caravans is coming to Uganda on 25 January to help our programme meet the increased demand for flights. For this reason Mike went to South Africa from 15 to 25 January in order to get the Caravan onto his South African pilot's licence. We praise and thank God for a safe trip, for successful training out there and for a chance to see his family. In February Mike flew a group of British MPs to the IDP camp in Gulu, where they spent the night. Thousands of 'night commuters' (children) come into Gulu each night to sleep rough on pavements, in doorways, etc. Their parents send them there so that they will not be abducted by the LRA during night raids on their villages. World Vision is one of the aid agencies that bring Christ's love into this awful situation. One of the ways God is victorious in the camps is that many folk are in a position to hear the gospel for the first time and many folk get to see the love of Christ in action.

We pray that 2006 is going well for you all and that you are all well. We want to thank you for the prayers, cards and letters you send us. Thank you for taking the time to care for us and encourage us.

Please praise God with us for:

- ❖ A wonderful Christmas and New Year, our first in Uganda.

- ❖ For the many safe flying and driving hours we have undertaken.

- ❖ New friends and good relationships within the MAF team.

- ❖ Mike's successful training in South Africa.

- ❖ Good health.

Please join us praying for:

- ❖ Steve and Iris of AIM as they adjust to life in Lokutok.

- ❖ The work of CBM and the Ruharo Hospital, Mbarara in particular.

- ❖ The safety and health of each team member.

- ❖ The elections due to be held in Uganda in late February.

- ❖ Cheriton Baptist Church, Kent, as they work to be His light in their area.

- ❖ John and Allie, as they look to God for guidance in their finances and future plans.

Please let us know how best to pray for you. Our heartfelt thanks to you and our heartfelt praise to God for you.

"You and your talents are not an accident. You are special in God's eyes. You have distinct gifts and talents. You have shoes to fill that no one else can wear." John Maxwell

"Keep me as the apple of your eye; hide me in the shadow of your wings." Psalm 17: 8

With our love and thanks,

Mike and Laura.

Lord, so much hangs on these elections! Your Word says that You place the leaders in power; please place the right person for Uganda in power. The needs here are so immense; the problems so many and so seemingly insurmountable; this person will need all the wisdom and help You alone can give.

Flying to Lokutok, I was suddenly aware of the many cups of tea I have the potential to have with many lady missionaries out here in Africa. Please help me to encourage them and please put time in my schedule to spend with them, wherever possible. It must be quite faith-stretching living so close to the LRA; I pray You not only protect missionaries doing so but that You also grant them peace as they entrust their safety to You. In Jesus' name, Amen.

Deborah and Ivan.

One day, whilst Mike was away flying, I took a group from church to Sanyu Babies' Home; I was the only one with a car! The church was helping out that day. The mummy in charge, a lovely lady called Joyce, asked me if I would ever consider adopting a child. My immediate reply was "no". Undeterred, she chatted to me about how Moses grew up in a foreign home and asked me to speak to Mike and to pray about it. Surrounded by 40 children, days old to 3 years old, my heart was breaking - how would one ever choose?! Anyhow, when Mike got back, we spoke and prayed about it; God showed us very clearly that this was His plan. So we asked Mummy Joyce to pick the child she felt would need us most. Joyce told us about Ivan, who would need a family soon as he was due to be moved on to an orphanage. Other folk had tried to take him, but he had refused to go. Ivan's best friend for the last two-and-a-half years had been Deborah. Well, on Good Friday, two little children, neither of whom spoke much English, left the hubbub and clamour of Sanyu and moved in with a rather odd couple who had a cat. Life changed overnight! The whole process happened in a matter of a week.

A note to God 15 October 2006

Lord, my family anchors me. In a good way! God you use them to train me in a multitude of ways. At times I soar, my heart bursting with enthusiasm, my mind running away with itself. They keep me in reality. They make my faith real and practical. It is so easy to be nice to a passing someone. It is easy to smile and be kind when you know that they are with you for a few hours or minutes. So much harder when they are with you always. Day in and day out.

Teach about the way of love. Try living it with 2 toddlers!

Preach on patience. Try not yelling at 2 toddlers when you are tired, hot and very bothered.

Teach on kindness. Try being kind when your son has pooed all over the sheets for the third day running.

I so love the time I have by myself. I enjoy hearing nothing, being alone, able to think and contemplate. I enjoy being 'on the mountain top'. But one has to come down sometimes and they make sure I do just that.

Time to read my Bible, to write to friends. So rare. Words and emotions pile up inside me, never finding the time to escape onto paper. So frustrating. So difficult not to have what you want all of the time. A lesson in sharing and caring. A way of developing self-discipline in time management, in letting go things that are important to you.

They teach me balance. Well, actually, I am still learning this along with all the rest.

Dreams and feelings. Pictures in my mind. Feelings in my heart; emotions so strong I want to cry in either joy or sadness. Faces. So many faces. Of young and old. Laughing, smiling, playing, desperate and afraid. All mixed together.

Sweeping scenery. Acacia trees, thorns and dust. Great, green belts and great, dusty plains. Rivers with fish eagles soaring above. Roads smothered in fumes, covered in litter and decaying canine corpses. Each roadside verge supporting a string of shacks where life is lived. Bananas and sodas, chicken grilled, shoes and pots and every other thing you can think of sold.

And this all in Your plan and in Your hands; wow!

News from Mike and Laura: 1 November 2006

Merry Christmas!

Dearest Friends and Family.

Our warmest greetings and much love to you all! Wow, what a year! So much has happened. We are now 4 instead of 2 as we spend our first Christmas as a family. As things work, Mike and Ivan will be in the UK from 27 November until 2 January so that Ivan can have his operation. So, we will be apart. But Mike will be with his sister and her family and their mum, and my mum will be coming for a week over Christmas, so all is well. Praise God for families!!! Mike and I have become so aware of how special it is to have a family as so many people around us have none. It has impressed upon us, once again, the amazing grace and love that there is in being a part of His family. We count each one of you as part of our wider 'family' and want to thank you for being there for us. So many prayers prayed, and each one answered. All healthy, all flights safely flown, all drives safely done; our marriage intact and happy (our third

Anniversary on 29 November!) and children settling-in well.

Now, a warning! :0) This is very much a 'loo-letter'. What we mean by this is that it is long, so leave it in the loo and read it bit by bit! Mike and I have been on some very special trips and we want to share with you what you, as a part of MAF and as a part of His family, make possible. We wish that you could be here to see it but, as you are missionaries where God has placed you, let us share with you what is happening here where He has placed us...

Where to begin? We live and work in an environment of great extremes...

Kalongo home-coming.

In mid-September Laura flew Dr Egidio from Kajjansi back to Kalongo, Northern Uganda. Dr Egidio, a Priest who has served in Kalongo for 17 years, was returning home after a 3-month furlough in Italy. The weather was atrocious, requiring much weaving about thunderstorms and the finding of safe passage through banks of cloud and torrential rain. As the aircraft touched down we could hear the singing, and see the bright colours of the pink and blue school shirts and the white of the nurses' uniforms. Around 200 people had come to meet the good doctor, waiting patiently and expectantly in the rain. One is not privileged so see this sort of thing very often. There before you a doctor with tears in his eyes, a smile that wrapped itself around his face, a joy bursting from deep within. A man with 17 years of his life lovingly woven into these very people. And these people, children and nurses, soldiers and herdsmen, have nothing. They have nothing to give, so they give themselves. Their time, their hearts, their love, and, most precious of all, their trust, all expressed in beautifully-sung songs and chants, great displays of cheering, dancing and drum-beating. Once in the car, we travelled a road lined with folk who had come out to greet him, each group singing him some or other special song. The doctor appeared overwhelmed with joy, overcome with happiness. He hugged and embraced each one who came, greeting each by name and in his or her own language, of which there appeared to be several. And you know that he does so much more than run a hospital of 350 beds. You want to cry because you realise you are seeing God at work, because someone and something very special is right there in front of you.

The week before you have flown a laboratory engineer up into the dangerous and remote Karamajong area of North-Eastern Uganda. You are driven through the most spectacularly stark area at breakneck speed in a car with the door falling off. You bounce past fields housing withered stalks of corn sulking beneath a washed-out blue sky bereft of rain, and arrive at the local 'clinic'. This comprises a small collection of half-derelict buildings and an acacia tree. Beneath the tree is a girl of around 5. She is covered in a shawl. Her skin is faded, her hair red and patchy from malnutrition. Unexpectedly, I hear a cry from beneath the shawl and discover that this child is caring for a baby which is only several weeks old. She tries to hush the baby but, hungry, it persists. I think of the squashed and hot sandwich I have in my bag. Do I give it to her or not? There are around 60 other people, many of them children, also waiting. You feel impotent, very unable, and very hollow. I try to talk to her but there is no understanding, so I put my hand on her shoulder and smile. You want to cry because you realise that you are seeing the slow death of a child as you hear God calling us to His work, because someone and something very special is dying right there in front of you.

Kigoma to Kalemie 31 Oct to 4 Nov 2006

Sometimes life throws a great adventure at you. Last week was such a time.

It was supposed to go like this: I was to fly Dr Larry and Sally Pepper (an American doctor with Southern Baptist Mission working at Mbarara hospital) from Entebbe to Kigoma, Tanzania. We were to be met by Azlin, who would drive us to the Baptist guesthouse and show us the boat he had arranged for the crossing of Lake Tanganyika the following day. 5 other folk, Rusty and Debbie Pugh from Kinshasa, and Tim Tidinberg and wife and daughter from Kenya, would fly in ahead of us from Kenya. I was to stay in the guest house for 4 days, relaxing and taking the odd swim in the lake. The weather would be sunny when we all flew back to Uganda on the Saturday.

The Southern Baptist Mission is looking to place a family in that part of the DRC in order to try and reach the mostly-unreached WaTabwa people. This trip was to be an initial mission look-see to this area.

This is how it really went...

The flight down went really well. The weather was OK, with all thunderstorms circumnavigable, one requiring a short foray into Burundi. Andy Blake, MAF Kigoma, was there to greet us. But no Azlin. We spent around an hour with immigration getting 2 passports stamped. Still no Azlin. So, into a taxi and off to the guesthouse. We never did see Azlin. The three of us headed off to the beach and there we found ourselves, sitting under a palm tree with an oven-hot breeze, eating fish-head and chips. The rest of the group arrived much later. 'Precision Air' turned out to be less precise than hoped for, arriving 4 hours late. The next day, Rusty was to discover that the Precision chicken sandwich was not quite as fresh as it should have been. Only three other folk arrived, Tim's wife and daughter staying on in Kenya.

As Azlin was nowhere to be found and had not arranged a boat (the group had hoped to sail that day), they spent the rest of the afternoon finding a boat. Initially the quote was $2,500, but it was finally negotiated to $700. It was available the next day and they would leave at 2pm. The trip would take 3 hours. I felt that this was, to say the least, optimistic, as the trip was 84nm direct and, whilst I don't know the first thing about boats, I was certain that the wooden ones on display would not reach the speed required.

The next day dawned and, having being invited to go with the group, I joined them in the long wait. The boat arrived at 3pm. We spent around an hour with immigration. Our boat was a large, wooden affair with a canopy made from UNHCR plastic. I put my lifejacket on. We set sail at around 4pm. 10 minutes out, the engine stopped. Our captain and his first mate quickly changed the spark-plugs and we were off again. 15 minutes out, the best mate started bailing water...

By 7pm the glorious pinks and golds had left the water and it was like sailing on ink. It was pitch black. There was not one light on the boat. I'd noted a Cumulonimbus thunderstorm cloud way out to the south of the lake and watched as it set off a chain reaction, spawning more CBs in a line that was on a converging path with us! The sky was no longer black - we were in the midst of a natural firework display! The waves and wind grew. I suddenly noted everyone else now had their lifejackets on as well! The captain finally decided to turn around. It was 11pm. Around 2 minutes later a blast of freezing cold air hit us from behind, lasting for around 5 minutes. We had turned around just in time. The sky above us was an angry orange; lightning and thunder drowned out the sound of our little 60hp outboard. We made it to a cove of a nearby island. As the lightning lit it up we saw rows of stone and thatch houses built into the rock - we were at Waterworld! Instantly little squares of light showed through the windows and folk of the WaGoma people came out shouting at us, telling us to go away as our boat would damage their fishing boats in the strong winds. Battling the waves, the captain got us to the next cove and we beached the boat onto the island. The men hopped out to find a bush and the ladies used the water-bailing bucket. By this stage we were all wet through. The wind shifted and so we raised anchor and setoff through the storm to the initial cove. Here the wind was now calm and so the people allowed us to stay. It was 1am. We all settled down on the wooden planks, trying not to touch the bottom of the boat, which was covered with water. We all slept in fits and starts. I was so cold that I woke myself up with the chattering of my teeth, raincoat and all! At first light we were off and it was 3 hours before we reached Kalemie Port. We passed the adjacent airport. We had been at sea for 18 hours; the flight would have been around 30 minutes.

I was immediately struck by the air of abandonment and decay. Rusting boats tied up alongside a rusting quay. A cargo boat, heavy laden and covered with standing

passengers, was just leaving, listing to port and way too heavy. Folk appeared from all over the place to look at this bedraggled set of *Muzungus*. It took 3 hours to get through Customs and Immigration. It was a very sad, very dirty place that smacked of dishonesty and despair.

Stephanie Hagenier came to pick us all up in her 4x4. Stephanie is a single missionary in her 40s who, with her mum and dad, who are in their 60s, runs a school for 1,200 children, together with a Bible college and a clinic for her staff. She is an amazing lady and has been there for 21 years. She speaks fluent French and Swahili and everyone there knows her and her parents. She showed Larry around the hospital, drove past various points of

interest and generally explained the ways of the city. She also provided a much-needed cup of coffee! All too soon our time was up. As we were about to set off, we noticed that one of the tyres was flat! Once that was fixed a call came through from the customs official and the 'game' had begun. We had hoped to set sail by 3pm. The tyre, together with belligerent officials hoping to make a quick buck, meant that, after much prayer and patient wrangling, we left at 6pm.

This time the trip took a mere 9 hours. We landed at 3am. Being 'British', I made a cup of tea for everyone before we all retired to our beds. Mine swayed the whole night through but did it feel soft after all those hours on wooden planks!

All told, it was thoroughly enjoyable! It is great to feel alive, to be in a situation where each sense is working at its maximum level, to be so very much aware that God is the one who is getting you all through this. It was very special to have a satellite phone on me and to be able to ask Mike to put out prayer chains. Thank you for praying for us. I was also able to mobile text message Mike our exact position every hour, which was a great encouragement to those on board. It also brought home to me the great work that God is doing and the great variety of people He uses. But of course there was one burning question: why didn't they fly!!!!?

By the way, the weather on the way back was fine.

Adventure in Wau.

Monday, 23 October 2006 was a very special day for me (Mike). Having felt for several months that the Lord was calling me to leave MAF and to stop flying, I felt an immediate peace once I had spoken to our boss and explained to him that I was leaving MAF. So, on the 23rd I found myself doing my last flight for MAF. It was with very mixed emotions that I watched Laura park her aircraft next to mine at Entebbe airport! But the Lord blessed me with one of the most amazing flights I had ever done!

I was to fly Dr Charles Price and some of his deacons, of Peoples' Church, Toronto, to Wau, Southern Sudan. He had been invited to speak there by the Bishop of the Anglican Church in that area. The weather was appalling and we ended up having to turn around half-way and land at Gulu, Uganda. We eventually managed to get into Arua after flying around bad weather and having lunch in Gulu! The night we spent in Arua ended up being a special time of fellowship whilst waiting one-and-a-half hours for our dinner of macaroni and tomato sauce. We got to know each other a lot better and shared about various aspects of our lives. Charles and his colleagues were so 'normal' and so 'real'. We had a lot of good laughs.

Having refuelled, we set off for Wau early Tuesday morning. The weather was fine and our flight to Wau was uneventful. Once there, we discovered why it was called Wau: our reaction to most things we saw was "WOW"! On final approach to land we could see various clapped-out old Russian aircraft lying in ruins, rusting away, next to the runway. Not terribly reassuring... This part of Sudan still bears a lot of the scars of war.

The airport authority then told us that the runway had been closed the whole of the previous day and, had we made it to Wau on the Monday, we would have been denied landing permission and had to return to Arua. It was so good to know that God was in the detail!

We were welcomed by Bishop Henry and most of his congregation, who all arrived to give us a special welcome at the airport. Charles was given a flower garland/necklace and so looked like he had just got off Aloha Airlines in Hawaii. (The only resemblance to Hawaii!)

The drive to the church was around 3km and we drove next to the tar road as it was much smoother. The church was in a walled-off area to the south of the city.

Around the church buildings, accommodation for orphans as well as schooling and teacher training facilities had been built. All this was very basic, being made out of sticks and woven palm leaves.

We were all welcomed into the church and I was immediately referred to as 'The White Dinka' because of my height and skinny look which resembles that of the Dinka people we were visiting in Sudan.

Bishop Henry told us that 2 years ago you could not walk on the street in Wau with a Bible in your hand, as you would have been arrested, beaten, etc. During the war 67 churches had been destroyed in this area alone. He had been imprisoned for 4 years. We later found out that almost 80% of the congregation had also been imprisoned because they were Christians. Charles preached the whole of Tuesday afternoon about St Paul in prison and his prison ministry, about how God works through us and not how we are working for God. His whole message was translated into both Dinka and Arabic by 2 different translators. The highlight of the message was when a bat flew in and landed on Charles' neck and crawled up the back of his hair! He did a frantic dance on the stage, much to the delighted amusement of the congregation, until the bat finally got fed up and flew off. I was very much aware that Charles had carefully and prayerfully thought about what he was going to preach and felt that it was very appropriate to the people there.

That evening Bishop Henry showed us around the church compound and pointed out one specific, large tree. It was on one the branches of this tree that Christians had been hanged for their faith.

That night we slept in the Bishop's lounge, as our hotel accommodation had been given to someone else! The duty rooster woke us all up at 4am. We all took turns in the one, cold shower, before heading off back to Uganda, very much awake.

Flying with Jesus Film Ministry.

On Wednesday, 15 November I met up with Sam Tsapwe of Jesus Film Ministry. Sam's mission is to share the love and life of Christ with as many people as possible by showing the Jesus Film, as well as several other Christian movies. Sam's heart is in this 101% and he often ventures out into remote and 'forgotten' places.

Well, the weather was great. We spent around 45 minutes squeezing a TV, generator, movie screens, a PA system, 50kg of New Testament Bibles in the local language, bags of clothes and a few treats for the children we would see, into the back of the C210. No need for gym that day! Both suitably hot and grubby, we launched off into the air, setting course for Gulu.

Gulu is well known outside of Uganda as a town of 'night commuters'. It has around 20 IDP camps, one alone containing approximately 65,000 refugees. Having negotiated with the military where I should leave the aircraft for the night, we off-loaded and headed into town.

Our first stop was the World Vision Children of War Rehab Centre. Sam and I spent around an hour listening to David Orone, the centre administrator, explaining to us how the centre worked. Their mission: "Our vision for every child: Life in all its fullness; our prayer for every heart: the will to make it so."

The centre opened in March 1995 and has since rehabilitated

15000 children who have escaped from the LRA. It also rehabilitates 'child-mothers'; that is, young girls abducted and forced to 'marry' LRA members, have had children and then have managed to escape.

 David shared how so many children are bitter and angry, feeling that they have no hope and no future. After escaping they spent 3 days being questioned by the military before being allowed to move on to the centre. They receive medical treatment, get given a 'welcome pack' containing various items, and they also receive counselling. They are normally there for around 2 months. The centre not only attempts to rehabilitate these children but it also attempts to fight against the stigma they have within their communities. They actively send out their personnel into the various communities and these folk try to get the community to forgive and accept the child back. I asked David if his family had been affected by the LRA and he said: "Yes, it has. In reality, I think 100% of the families in this area have been affected by the LRA." The centre readily recognises that

it is restoring the dreams of the children through partnership with the Ugandan army, the UN and various other partners. I left with a fresh respect for all these people; those fighting to help children recover and build a new life, as well as the children themselves, who have so much to work through and overcome.

We then met up with several people of Lifeline Ministry Church, Gulu. They were an enthusiastic, on-fire-for-the-Lord bunch, who promptly bundled Sam and I into a *mutatu* and set off to the Unyama IDP camp. The clouds had gathered and a few drops were already fallingas we bounced our way through big puddles left over from yesterday's rain. We suddenly found the vehicle surrounded by hundreds of children, pouring out from round, thatched huts, popping up from behind bushes and scampering down trees. After some careful negotiation, we found a site (under a jack-fruit tree!) to set up the TV, PA system, etc. and set about getting things ready. It rained. They stayed. Finally the movie

started. There was Sam explaining to the Gulu pastor what to say as the Gulu pastor translated the movie into the local language. 10 minutes later and it started to pour down! All hands on deck as bits were unplugged and our jackets thrown over delicate electrical equipment. But,

well, guess what? People started coming up and asking to be 'saved'! They asked to have Jesus in their hearts! God was at work, even in the pouring rain! Even when the movie restarted, children came up to Mary (a wonderful 'mother' on the Lifeline team) and we just stood and prayed for youngsters as they asked to have Jesus in their lives. Around 100 people came to know Christ as their personal Saviour in that camp. Who would have thought it? The rain, the mud, the lack of clear language, the noise of the thunder. All drowned out by the might and love of the Holy Spirit. I got back into that *mutatu* with this glorious picture in my head of thousands of angels singing upstairs with total delight!!! Matthew 5:6

"Blessed are those who hunger and thirst for righteousness for they WILL be filled."

All aboard for the next stop which was the Lifeline Church back in Gulu town. We arrived (late by an hour but it didn't matter - folk were just singing praises so loudly that the rafters shuddered...) and unpacked, setup and joined in the singing. Sam was showing a movie on Transformation. It showed 4 different towns on 3 continents that had undergone radical transformation when the churches had all got together and prayed. We shared from the Word what the Lord had laid on our hearts about Gulu, knowing that these brothers and sisters in Christ are the salt and light in their area and hoping to encourage them as they had done us. It was near 11pm when I finally got to bed.

0620hrs and the phone is ringing! What?!!! It was the airfield manager at Gulu. There had been a last minute change in the military schedule and I had to come and move my aircraft. Well, I can confidently vouch for the fact that finding a taxi is not easy! It arrived at 8am. Ah, well. So Sam, Sam2, a local pastor whose mother had just been admitted into hospital in Soroti, and I set off for the airfield. I was escorted to the military side of Gulu to fetch the C210 and told not to look at anything... We all set off for Lira, where we said goodbye to Sam2 and a big hello to Michael, the Director of Studies at the Lira Integrated School. He was busy with exams so came back to fetch us at 3pm. Sam didn't waste any time! He got chatting to 3 youths sitting watching some very dubious music show on TV. Out came the Bible and we shared the Good News. All 3 of these men asked Christ into their hearts! We wanted to give each a Bible, so we asked if we could take 3 Gideon Bibles from the B&B and replace them the next day. So it was a call to Richard in the MAF office, who found the Bibles and sent them up on the next aircraft. What a team! So, these 3 chaps set off back to their village by bicycle with the Bibles wrapped up in a plastic bag, telling us how they were going to tell others in their village about this Jesus… A pointed reminder to me, a somewhat over-punctual, task-orientated person, about the value of being made to wait sometimes!!!

At 3pm we set off to the school. We'd been asked to speak to 2 different groups of youngsters and then Sam would show 'Pamela's Prayer', a movie dealing with purity, that evening.

The first group comprised around 120 'special needs' children. They were mostly 'street-children' and former abductees. We walked into a small classroom where children were sat 3 to a desk. They ranged from around 6 to 16. I saw one small smile from a little boy up front.

The group seemed dejected and thoroughly miserable. Sam and I shared with them what the Lord had laid on our hearts. With a conviction of heart, mind and soul, I told them how God had created them, how they were precious, special and loved by Him. I asked them what they wanted most. They all replied: "A good life". We then asked who would like prayer, explaining that we would come to each of them in turn as they wanted. Dozens of hands went up. It is one of those poignant memories I will always carry with me; there, kneeling next to desk after desk, little arms creeping their way around me as we prayed for relief from nightmares, headaches, spirits tormenting them, guilt over what they had done, trauma over what they had seen, fear and despair. Several asked Jesus into their lives. And then, quite suddenly, time had run out and we were asked to move on. As I left, a youth of around 15 came up to me and thrust a carefully-scrawled note into my hand. One of his eyes was missing and the other had a slash through it. His shaved head readily revealed a large dent in his skull. His eye shone and there was a smile on his face. He wanted Jesus and so there, in front of all his friends, he asked Christ into his heart. The note reads: "I, Okuir Jimmy from Uganda, I would like to thank God for making you a chance to come and feed us with the word of God in Uganda, in particular Lira Integrated School. Your friend, Jimmy." So, next time you wonder whether the prayers and support you give to MAF actually make a difference, or you drop the spanner on your toe in the hangar, or the network crashes, or there are too many 'fires' for even the London Fire Brigade to put out, the kids are sick and the water is off, or the weather is bad and you wonder what on earth you are part of MAF for...

We walked over to the school hall. There were around 500 children there, all singing and dancing about. It was 'fellowship' time. The school is unashamedly Christian, PTL! They sang and danced. Sam and I shared with them as well. A loud 'gong' at 6pm signalled dinner-time and they were done in a flash. After dinner, Sam showed the movie and was there until way past 10pm. The children had been so moved. 69 of them asked Jesus into their lives.

That night I had dreams in which the children came to me in great distress, so I prayed to God to wake me up and He did. I realized yet again that, regardless of how bleak and terrible something looks to man, to God all things are redeemable. Each and every situation, no matter how terrible, He can use and redeem to His glory.

I met so many amazing Ugandan people. Sam works with a deep passion and a total dedication. His family spend a lot of time without him and a lot of time waiting for him. Their hearts are in the ministry, too! Teachers, carers, pastors, 'mothers'... each of these folk so kind, patient and dedicated to Christ.

His love and His power shine with an unquenchable power through the darkness. He is, quite simply, unconquerable. He is the answer to all things and each time we are kind, we love, we are patient, etc., we bring His Kingdom into the present.

And so it remains to thank you all yet once again. We could not have done it without you! God has surely blessed us. We met up with many of you in July, have received some wonderfully uplifting emails and letters, the kids have been treated to unexpected love-parcels, we reached 65% of our fundraising target this year and we have both grown in our faith. May the Lord bless you all and give you a wonderful Christmas and a 2007 that brings you much joy and happiness.

Our love, Mike, Deborah, Ivan and Laura.

"Glory to God in the highest, and peace on earth to men on whom His favour rests." Luke 2:14

"For my eyes have seen your salvation… a light for revelation to the Gentiles…" Luke 2:30

Lord, I may not always agree with everything I see or with everything other folk may do, but I do stand in awe of their hearts and their commitment! Thank You for showing me that You see the heart, not what the world sees.

Mike has stopped flying and this is difficult for me to understand. I know that he knows You have led him this way so I have to honour his decision. Show me how to support him in this as he sets out on the new path You have called him to walk. Thank You that we got to do his last flight 'together'. I think of the children I have met who have been so traumatised and I cannot help but think that it could so easily have been Deborah and Ivan. Lord, thank you for them both, that they are with us. Help Mike and me as we parent them: we have so much to learn! In Jesus' name, Amen.

The week that was...
5 December 2006

On Wednesday I had a challenging day! I got airborne for Entebbe where I was to pick up 2 ladies who were flying in from Seattle, USA. About two-and-a-half miles out a red light came on; the alternator had failed. So, it was back to Kajjansi. Around 45 minutes later I was off to Entebbe again. I picked up the 2 rather jet-lagged ladies and taxied out, only to find that I now had a fault with the right magneto. So, it was back to Kajjansi. The engineers were 'all hands on deck', no doubt wondering what I would break next!!! We eventually left (Michael Mukasa having organised a cup of coffee for the ladies) for Bundibugyo. On landing, the aircraft got firmly stuck in the mud. Praise God that the propeller did not strike the ground. Nevertheless, it took much pushing, heaving and shoving and around 3 hours to get the aircraft out. There was no way that I would be able to depart off that runway so I informed the doctor whom I was due to fly out that we would not be able to leave. No sooner had I told him this than his phone rang. It was the hospital - if he hadn't left would he please come back as there was a critically-ill lady who desperately needed his attention?

Dr Jonah operated on her until 10pm that night. He told us the next day that he felt it was divine intervention as, had we left, the lady would have surely died. I was concerned for Deborah but the MAF family took good care of her! Hadija took her home that night and the Forsythes had her on Thursday night until I got back. Becky played 'dress up' with her and Jessica cooked extra pasta to feed us all.

On Friday Sam, David, Moses, Deborah and I flew to Mbarara. It was a 2-hour drive to Rushere where we met a great group of people who had been eagerly anticipating Sam's arrival. We ate (of course!) and then all piled into the mud-and-wattle church, where members of the congregation were singing their hearts out. Drums, whistles and a harmonica! Lots of dancing and clapping; Ankole music is very infectious! We spoke about the role and characteristics of the Church, before dancing and singing some more. David and Moses got all technical and set up the sound system and DVD player, whilst Deborah and her new-found friend danced and jumped up and down. Sam showed *The Passion*. Many people were deeply moved by the film and many cried. One lady wept almost the whole way through, repeatedly asking: "What are they doing to my Lord?" It was a special time for Sam, who was returning to this group of friends after a long absence. There was a 10pm curfew due to insecurity in the area, and so special permission was obtained to 'stay late'. The film ended around 0030hrs; we made our accommodation at around 0100hrs only to find 'the big bad wolf with her hair on fire' sleeping in our bed! (I'd have been the same had someone walked into my room at 1am!) Mercifully Sam had 2 tents so, by

0145hrs, Deborah and I were 'lights out'. Of course it rained, for those of you wondering…

It was a reminder of how special the MAF family is; a big "thank you" to everyone in the hangar and Ops for working so hard to fix all the problems, to those in the office who looked after Deborah, and to 'Jinja' (Hadija) for taking her home and spoiling her.

News from Mike and Laura: January 2007

I have spent most of the morning in bed. The sun has been streaming through my window and I have watched an enormous thunderstorm slowly sail past. Having tonsillitis has its benefits! At 6am, once I'd decided that there was no way I was going to be able to fly today, I had to awaken my colleague, Gerrit, and ask him to do my flight. He was exceedingly gracious, especially for that time of day! Mike got the children ready and I listened to how happy there were, burbling and chattering away as Mike, as usual, kept all things calm and peaceful. It was good to be reminded of how blessed I am to have family and MAF colleagues here who are Godly and loving.

MAF was very busy over December. It had some unusual challenges!

The first one was getting the aircraft stuck in the mud! Thanks to all of you who prayed for us that day; you never know what you are praying for but that day it was most needed! I got airborne and had an alternator failure so returned to base. Once fixed, I tried again, only to have a magneto failure and needed to get that fixed. Finally, we got airborne for Bundibugyo, in the far west of Uganda. I inspected the runway from the air and it looked fine. We'd had a verbal confirmation on the suitability of the airstrip from the folks on the ground by phone earlier that day. Well, I landed and we got stuck. So after much pushing and shoving on wooden boards, the World Harvest Mission (WHM) team and I managed to get her out. We provided all the passers-by with hours of free entertainment! Mike was in the UK with Ivan and so I needed to get someone to look after Deborah for the night, as it was getting dark and I was unable to fly back. I'd like to say that I didn't worry about her but I did, as initially she refused to go with the MAF lady, even though she knows her well. I was due to fly a doctor out and had to explain that we would only be able to go the following day. Well, no sooner had the words left my mouth than his phone rang. It was the hospital. If he was still on the ground, could he come ASAP as he was urgently needed? A lady had given birth by caesarean section 2 days before and had suddenly fallen very ill. By the time the doctor got to her she was so ill that he had to operate on her under local anaesthetic. He worked on her until 10pm that night and saved her life. He called the next day to tell us that he believed that God's hand was in us getting stuck! I was reminded of how God promises to work all things for our good and to His glory.

That weekend held the second adventure. I flew Sam Tsapwe, his 2 teenage sons and Deborah down to Mbarara. We all squeezed into a little car, sitting cheek by jowl with PA systems and copies of the Jesus movie, and spent 2 hours bouncing along a dirt track to a village called Rushere. It was fantastic. The people were so friendly, so hungry for the Gospel, so excited to have us all there. Deborah danced away with all the other little children and had a wonderful time. Security in that area is not the greatest and so there was a 10pm curfew. The local pastor managed to get permission for us to minister on into the early hours of the night. We pitched our tents at 1am, in the rain (of course...) and were up at 6am. Many people were touched by the movie and what we shared with them. We were very moved by their hospitality, generosity and love. All of us left touched by God's love.

Christmastime can be quite a tough time as, generally, family and friends are miles away, you miss the 'cold' Christmas with turkey and one hardly notices it is happening over here. But many of us had family come to visit. My mum came for a week over Christmas and was thrown into the deep end of life here! I'd decided to take her and Deborah to Jinja (just 2 hours down the road) for the weekend. We had a great time and felt most relaxed looking out over the River Nile. On the way home, however, one of the front-wheel bearings broke! Several mobile phone calls later to Mike in the UK, covered in grease and very hot, I had to concede defeat and we got towed home! We'd looked at B & Bs but, being Christmas Eve, there was - you got it - no room in the inn!!!

It was a reminder that God has His plans, that we don't always know what they are, and that we have to be content with that. On 27 December I was asked to medevac a seriously-ill lady out of Fort Portal. She had pregnancy complications and needed to get to a hospital ASAP. The operations staff swung into action; I jumped into my uniform and dashed off to the office to phone for the weather. Fort Portal is a small village 6100ft above sea level, hugged up against a huge mountain range in the far west of Uganda. The weather was terrible and we couldn't fly in, so we arranged to pick her up early the next day. Having pre-flighted the aircraft, I was called by the programme manager to say that the weather was still too bad and that the lady would now come by car. A one-and-a-half-hour round trip by air would now take the best part of 10 hours by road. Please do pray for the many missionaries around the world who have to face such testing times as did this lady and her husband this Christmas.

3 January was a happy day! Mike and Ivan returned from a 5-week stay in the UK. Well, I can tell you that 5 weeks

can be a very long time! Thank you for the many prayers and cards you sent. Being apart for our wedding anniversary, Christmas and New Year was made that much more bearable by having so many cards and gifts appear in the post! Mike and Ivan had gone home so that Ivan could have an operation at Great Ormond Street Hospital. We were told that his testes would not descend. He left Uganda with them 'up' and arrived at the hospital to meet the consultant with them 'down'. What an answer to prayer! Mike and I believe that God worked a miraculous healing in Ivan. We know that many of you were praying for him and the rest of our family. May we encourage you by God's answer to your prayers and also thank you for your faithfulness and your care? We serve a God who hears and who sees and who cares!

Mike's sister and her husband were due to have their first baby on 24 December so we decided that Mike and Ivan would stay to see the little one. Well, she kept us waiting! Mike and Ivan left at midday on 2 January and the little miss arrived at 0007hrs on 2 January! We had prayed that Mike would get to see the baby and, well, God is just so good, because he and Ivan (intrigued to find a baby that was in the tummy now out of the tummy!) got to see the little girl. She was named Yasmin.

Many of you have asked what Mike is doing now that he is no longer flying. Well, Mike has a very special and gentle nature which children just adore, and so Mike has decided to stay at home with the children for the meantime. Deborah and Ivan adore him and are thrilled he is around all the time. (We pitched a tent in the garden which we are all sleeping in tonight!) Mike is praying about his future as he has a heart for children and there are so many here that need some love. He has spent many hours in a government office this last week (8 trips in all) obtaining one piece of paper for a Christian couple setting up a training centre in Kitgum for LRA escapees. We value your prayers for us at this time of change and adjustment.

On 4 January, Far Reaching Ministries, Sudan, called us to ask us to do a medevac for them. One of their American staff in the Sudan had leukaemia, had become very distressed, refusing to eat, and needed to get back to America ASAP. I wondered what I'd say to the man once I got there but, because He is faithful, God gave me the words (Exodus 4:12!), and so we prayed together for some time before I flew him to Entebbe. I can honestly say that he stepped out of the aircraft with a smile and reassured, simply because God cares and had made it possible for him to get flown out by MAF. Being a MAF pilot certainly is never the same 2 days running. Mike and I believe that God honours all the prayers you pray for us as we always manage to get through these kinds of situations. We pray that you find encouragement from these stories and realise how vital the work of MAF, of which you are an integral part, really is.

And, just to end, two more examples of the work folk from all over, of all races and ages, are doing to spread the gospel, getting there by folk like you who make it possible for MAF to fly them to the remote and dangerous parts of Sudan...

We flew Sam Tsapwe of Jesus Film Ministry, a dentist and a dental technician up to Iquitos, Sudan, in early January and brought them back a few days later. When I picked them up they were all decorated with garlands of flowers and just so excited and so thrilled at the people they had met, the work (both dental and spiritual) that God had done through them, and just the whole

experience. At the altar-call after the first movie shown, every person came forward and asked Jesus into their heart, PRAISE GOD!

The next day I flew Ken Matthews (SIL, SUDAN) up to Kapoeta. This is a very dangerous part of Sudan in the 'Red' UN zone, so that flying is the safest option. Ken and his wife are living in Lira, Uganda. They founded and 'run' (from the background, Ken was keen to point out) the Fountain Primary School. They have been spending 3 months each year in Lira for the last 8 years, and moved there permanently over a year ago. They are sponsored by the Family Church in Bournemouth. They have 28 children of the Taposa Tribe, near Kapoeta, Sudan (similar and related to the Karamajong and Masaai peoples) coming to school in Lira! They sponsor 16 of the children and the local Kapoeta commissioners sponsor the other 12. Initially the commissioners did not want girls to get educated, but

Ken spoke with them and explained the benefits and so they agreed. At the end of last term they bussed the children all the way from Lira back to Kapoeta. The soldiers at the border ordered all the children off the bus to get caned, as they were Taposa and not Dinka and there is a lot of friction between the two tribes. Ken says that they spent a very tense 2 hours at the border! Ken asks for prayer whilst in Kapoeta because it is in the red security zone and he needs to travel way outside the main village into the outlying villages. His team is trying to help the local Christians set up a church there: when I landed the only 'standing' structure I saw was a huge mosque, so please do pray.

On the same flight I also flew Chuck Banks (Calvary chapel, USA) and his granddaughter, Drena Banks, to Nimule, Sudan. Drena is 10 years old and will be doing children's and women's ministry! I marvelled at the faith of her grandfather bringing her to Sudan (she lives with them permanently). He has been on two short-term missions already and this was his third visit. Drena was so excited! They are working with FRM on this trip.

We have so much to praise Him for. Thank you all so much for your faithful prayers, support and love.

Praise for:

- ❖ Ivan being healed.

- ❖ Yasmin being born healthy and mum (and dad!) both well after the experience.

- ❖ The joy and gift of family and friends.

- ❖ The many missionaries out here spreading the Gospel of God's love.

- ❖ The amazing work of Jesus Film Ministry and Sam Tsapwe.

Prayers for:

- ❖ Laura's upcoming annual flight exams (practical and oral) in March; the whole family is going to South Africa for this so please pray for a safe trip, for a special time as many family members meet the children for the first time, and for exam success.

- ❖ Upcoming weekend trips with Jesus Film Ministries: for wisdom, sensitivity to their needs and a real guiding by the Holy Spirit.

- ❖ Continued safety as we drive on very unsafe roads and fly in challenging weather conditions.

- ❖ We have been assigned August for furlough this year; please pray that God will guide us in the planning of this.

Thank you again for taking this journey with us. Please do let us know if we can pray for you or your church in any way. Please do put return addresses on letters so that we can write back to you. With much love to you all, God bless,

Mike, Ivan, Deborah and Laura.

"He was delivered over to death for our sins and raised to life for our justification." Romans 4:25

Dear Kate

This is quite a difficult thing to write about because I haven't quite managed to process it all. A weekend like this leaves many memories and feelings and emotions that I simply cannot instantly come to grips with. It is hard to find the words, and even harder to write with an unbiased integrity that reflects the reality as it is and not merely as I feel and perceive it. What I can say is that to see people who live in such grinding poverty, under such oppression and yet have such hope and faith, is a truly humbling experience. It is they who should be the missionaries in the UK!

It seems quite surreal, sitting here in my house in Kampala writing to you about this last weekend with Jesus Film Ministry. I am on a soft bed, having had a really good meal with a hot bath yet to come. I will go to sleep tonight with a security guard pacing about outside. I won't need to worry about my husband or kids being abducted. I won't need to get up at sunrise, start a fire and then beat sheaves of millet to get the grain out. I got back on Sunday and that night I really struggled to 'adjust'- the 1-hour flight takes you from one world into another and the time-frame is not long enough for my brain to adjust!

Friday morning I met Pastor John-Graham of Frontline Ministries, Mukono (about 30km east of Kampala.) He is around 30 and has been on many trips with Sam. He had never flown before and, like Sam, had never been to Pader before. As we were preparing to leave, a huge thunderstorm was brewing. Angry black clouds poured over the hills, attempting to drown Kajjansi. It was as if Satan was saying: "You're going nowhere". But God is faithful and His hand simply swept the huge system aside. We were met at Pader by Pastor Dennis (Lifeline Ministries) who bundled us all into a World Vision van that they had lent him for a few hours. Pader is a pretty out-of-the-way place. It is/was a stronghold of Kony, having been the preferred area for many of his shrines. It is basically a large, dirt road, with various bars where folk can drown their sorrows, and stalls either side, that runs through an IDP camp. Our first stop was the pastor's home, a small concrete-and-mud brick room. He slept on the floor that night so that Sam could sleep on his bed. I then met Katie, who lives in a room in the IDP camp. I got to see and live a small part of IDP life for the day. It is a town with very little Christian input and very few Christian NGOs. Sam's was the first Christian team I had ever flown in there. The next stop was the local police HQ, where we met and chatted with the chief policeman. He gave us permission to show the movie and asked if we could come back to show it in the surrounding IDP camps. He was not a Christian, but did say that God answered all his prayers. He told us that they all work 7 days a week. I asked if they had a chaplain there and he said no. We walked back from his office up a long hill in the baking heat, all pouring with sweat and covered in dust. Huts, brick-works and crops. Bicycles and cows; no cars. No electricity whatsoever unless it was solar or generator. We had lunch at a restaurant that is staffed and run by women who are former abductees. They have no education and so this initiative (by the local church) is a lifeline to them. People were very wary of photos and so I didn't manage to take many.

That night, Friday, was, by coincidence, the start of a traditional dancing weekend. The local lads and lasses dance bare-chested in order to pick up partners. Immorality is rampant in this camp and hurts the ladies the most as they are left with a baby and the man moves on. HIV/AIDS is also a huge problem. They were due to perform right alongside us. So, we set up the outdoor screen, projector and sound system on the dirt soccer field and prayed. As usual, it was the children who got there first. 5 or so. Then adults. Soon enough we were surrounded by around 500 people, all desperate to see the Jesus movie. Not one person danced that night or the rest of the weekend. So many people asked Christ into their lives that Sam lost count. The pastor called on Sunday night to say that his church had been packed that Sunday. It was truly a night for God and it was truly His night.

My evening in the hut was a humbling one. I had to be shown how best to do everything! Katie would say:" No, don't take all this to the washroom, just take this." The washroom is a communal one. It consists of a rough mud floor surrounded by corrugated iron and wood bits that reach just above waist height, with huge gaps in. Being a *mzungu* I naturally drew a crowd! So there I was, trying to bath with 2 litres of water in a bucket and not get seen!

Dozens of children, passing pooches, you name it, and there they were.

Katie's room is about 1.5m X 2m and her whole world is in it. Her few items of clothing hang on nails bashed into the wall. A bed serves as sofa, bed and storage unit. A small table is kitchen. She had a small packet of sugar, half a cup of tea-leaves, a small tin of milk powder and around 4 handfuls of biscuit-bites. She made me tea using a very small Primus stove, at which point I discovered that she was fasting and praying about our trip there! Katie insisted I slept on her bed; she borrowed a mattress off a neighbour and slept on the floor. The small, glassless but barred window and the door were both locked for security. I slept soundly, awoken by the duty rooster. Outside, ladies were cooking, children sweeping or fetching water, dogs snoozing and a man was building a hut alongside. A lady arrived with her 8-month-old baby, Krist. He was ill with malaria. So I prayed for them. She was around 22; the man had run off, she had no job. Katie then asked if I would pray with her as she hadn't been paid since last year and things were getting desperate. She works for a CHRISTIAN group and I just felt so angry! Having just read through *James* that morning (God knew what was coming!) I was able to share and encourage her. It is hard to see someone oppressed and starved, especially by a Christian group. Katie works 7 days a week as a financial administrator. She is from Kampala, and came to Pader to work for this Christian group at great personal risk and cost to herself. The group helps widows and orphans. Quite suddenly our transport to the airstrip was there and we were off. I was dirtier, smellier and my uniform was a lot more crumpled than usual. But nothing compared to how crumpled my heart felt for these folk who really do live the Gospel, who really do suffer for His name's sake, who really do show Christ to their community and to passers-by like me.

The weather on Saturday was perfect. It was a 20-minute flight to Gulu. I dropped the team off at the civilian side and then taxied the aircraft around to the military side (at their insistence). A Russian helicopter had just landed so there was quite a tense atmosphere. A Russian instructor was on board so I managed to recall a few words of Russian and chat with him. One is painfully aware that MAF is on trial by what we do, say and how we act and that there is chance to witness on each meeting. I am sorry to say that I don't always do that well, but thank God that He was with me that day and that it all went well. The 'negotiations' took a good 30 minutes and so we spent the rest of the day chasing time.

Our first stop was a school for war children - 673 of them. A large hall with tin roof and several hundred bodies meant that every single one of us was pouring with sweat within minutes. The children had been waiting patiently for 3 hours! We managed to have them all laughing within seconds of me trying to teach them a song (nope, singing is not my gift!!!) We gave our testimonies and Sam shared many things with them. They all watched the movie and at least 50 children asked Christ into their hearts that day. One of the little girls, around 4 years old, wanted to come home with me. I had to walk away. It breaks your heart. You come, you go, and they stay. It is hard to imagine what they have seen and been through. My consolation is in knowing that

God promises to always defend the poor, the fatherless and the oppressed and that He really does love each and every one of them.

I had not eaten since lunch the day before, so I was really getting to see what life up there was like. One meal a day is a privilege. We didn't stop for lunch but moved straight on to a church in a rough area of Gulu. We had the equipment up in 10 minutes. In that time we were surrounded by children, all eager to see the movie. What strikes one is how the 4-, 5- and 6-year-olds are all carrying small babies. They (normally girls, unless there are only boys in the family) have real responsibilities from a really early age. We showed the movie and, once again, many folk gave their hearts to the Lord. It was 6pm when we left for the hotel where we were to stay that night. We had a meal (I was ready to eat whatever they had by this point! Black chunks of something in a beige sauce and millet), and then Sam set off for the same church to show another movie at 7.30pm. Around 1,000 people crammed into that church, and many gave their hearts to the Lord.

On Sunday morning we were picked up for the 7am service. Well, blow-your-socks-off stuff it was. The praise and worship went straight through you! The pastor of that church (Sam of Lifeline Ministries) had just returned from Kampala. He had been severely ill with malaria, and yet there he was jumping about and singing his heart out. He was just so thrilled that we had come back (we visited them around 2 months ago) and the church treated us like old friends. Once again we shared what the Lord had laid upon our hearts, showed a movie and then it was time to leave.

Many folk were reached. Many heard the Gospel for the first time. Many people felt that they mattered, that someone out there cared. As always, it was a huge team effort. Our spouses are left with the children and they are both aware that we are not always in the safest of places. Our MAF aircraft handlers file flight plans, refuel and worked really hard on the Friday to make the trip a success. Someone has to flight-follow and this, on a weekend (we do not normally fly on Sundays as this really does impact on many folk), is a real sacrifice. MAF has a lot of people involved in each flight, not just the pilot. It was this team that, together with the many faithful MAF prayer and financial supporters, made it possible for hundreds of men, women and children living in the most desperate of circumstances, to hear about the love of Christ. Thank you to each person who made it possible, and all glory to God in the highest.

Lira with Jesus Film Ministry and Family: 1 April 2007

Sam Tspawe, Jesus Film Ministry and the Bundy-Westleys all flew up to Lira on the Friday. We were on a 4-day trip back to this town that is situated around midpoint Uganda. Sam and I had been there a few months previously and wanted to re-visit the children of Lira Integrated School whom we had met on our first trip. This was one of the main reasons for this trip, as we both felt that we needed to see them again to see how they were doing and how best we could encourage them. It was to prove to be a challenging, encouraging and, at times, demoralizing 4 days.

Whilst we knew that we were to visit the school, the rest of the time had been planned for us so there was a real element of surprise to our stay! Once in Lira, we had an early lunch and then the 5 of us headed off to one of the churches with our on-the-ground contact in Lira, Jonathan. Jonathan is a teacher at the Lira Integrated School as well as a pastor in one of the Lira churches. He told us that he had arranged a weekend conference-cum-retreat for leaders from the surrounding area. The pastors and other church leaders (finance, youth pastors, women's ministry leaders, etc.) were coming from as far as the Karamajong border. The first part of the conference was in a very modest mud-and-stick church, complete with tin roof and dung floor. Christmas decorations and small strips of coloured cloth festooned the interior of the building. Initially there were around 5 ladies and 10 children, but we were soon bursting at the seams! Handmade musical instruments of all kinds, drums, whistles and many voices and stamping feet joined together to raise huge clouds of dust and praise that could not have failed to reach Heaven!

Sam was to show the Transformation movie and I was to speak. The movie shows the amazing impact on 4 different cities on 3 continents that the working, praying and coming together of all the churches in that area brought about. We are talking about whole communities being transformed; out of drugs, witchcraft, violence, etc. and into peaceful and thriving cities! I spoke on the responsibilities that leaders have, encouraging the leaders present to resist the temptation to abuse their power, the temptation to see themselves as more important and of a higher status. Sam and I both recognise that there is much abuse of power, and that many leaders treat those they lead with very little respect and love so this, we felt, was the right message.

At the end of the day we walked back to the hotel, picking our way through the trash and debris that residents in the slums live alongside. It is not hard to see why infant mortality runs at 35% and life expectancy is 50.

On Saturday we all went to another church. This church was nestled in the midst of a tranquil village. Thatched huts, cows, chickens and goats, dozens of children playing happily together under mango trees, a gentle breeze, and a clear blue sky. We were given a wonderful welcome as villagers came out singing and waving flowers. Deborah instantly learnt how to ululate and was whisked away by the ladies, smiling from ear to ear. The church was packed. As the day wore on, more and more folk crammed in! You cannot go to church in Uganda and not dance and sing. Here they jump, too! So we all jumped and sang and jumped and sang some more, until the sweat poured off every single person there! Sam felt that the right movie to show was the Jesus movie, which he showed once I had spoken with the leaders. I encouraged the leaders to 'tend their doctrinal gardens' and encouraged the leaders to research and think about what they were actually preaching and teaching, as Sam and I were both concerned with the growing number of folk teaching unbiblical/unscriptural things. After the movie, Sam spent a lot of time encouraging the people. Many who were not leaders had also come, and many accepted Christ into their lives. Ivan and Deborah had a fantastic time playing with the other children, touching their first cow and being chased by the chickens!

On Sunday, Palm Sunday, Sam headed off to a church with Jonathan whilst Mike, the children and I went to the Lira Integrated School. Both Mike and I got all choked up as we watched and heard the several hundred children sing praises to God; I could almost see Him sitting up there in Heaven smiling with joy! We had the whole day with the children. The first part of the day was 'church'. Ivan and Deborah had a great time singing and dancing along. For the 'sermon' part, I grabbed various children from the group and we all acted-out John Chapter 9. I explained to them that it was Jesus who went and found the young man who had been thrown out of the synagogue and not the other way round, and that Jesus seeks each one of us out; that Jesus has sought Mike, D & I and me out and that He seeks them out, too. Once 'church' was done, the main group left whilst those children from the 'bush' remained. I spent some time talking with them, letting them talk and ask questions, sharing the Gospel. We did this in an informal group, sitting on chair-backs and 'hanging out' whilst D & I walked amongst them asking them what their names were! We then asked who wanted prayer and Mike and I prayed for many of the children. At 11am they went off for breakfast! It was good to be able to speak with them 'outside', to hear some of their stories, to just be there with them. All they want is someone to visit, someone who knows that they exist, and someone who cares even just a little bit. It was intensely frustrating at times, too. Faeces covered the un-flushed toilets. Everything was dirty and uncared for. The children seemed to lack any sense of self-worth. We saw a teacher hit a boy on the head with a stick. We saw many children shouted at for no apparent reason; children did not appear to be treated with any dignity. Children have to bow down each time a teacher passes by and, whilst this is cultural to an extent, it showed us that there is very much an authoritarian air about the place. We did not see a child run up to a teacher and show affection or happiness. We saw children afraid of their teachers, unable to express any opinion. There are many good teachers and many loving teachers, we are sure, it's just that we didn't see them that afternoon. That afternoon we all gathered in the hall and shared and sang some more. Sam arrived at 4pm and so we passed the baton on to him. Sam shared his testimony with them and showed a movie. They were thrilled! Many children asked Christ into their hearts.

So, what to say to it all? Mike and I have spent many hours thinking about all of this. As God Himself seeks out each of us one by one, the best we can do is help one person at a time. Please do pray for the children in the many hundreds of boarding schools in Uganda. Please pray for their teachers. Please pray for those like Sam who share the Gospel, the only true hope for them and us. I have a list of children who need various things like panties, toilet paper, sanitary pads (girls are using newspaper at the moment), books, pencils, etc. Please let me know if you would like to help in any way, write a letter to them, etc.

News from Mike and Laura: May 2007

I have decided that there is something to be said for the 'nanny state'! For those of you who don't follow the Royal goings-on, The Queen is visiting Uganda in November, along with the other members of The Commonwealth. This has turned Kampala into something of a building site. Skyscrapers are being erected, all via rickety wooden scaffolding, at an amazing rate. Roads are being dug up, lands seized, deals done. 'Health and Safety' is non-existent and folk clamber about quite fearlessly and often oblivious to the dangers. As this Third World country clambers to move on from where she is, many fall victims to the lack of safety rules and regulations. We all cough almost continuously because of the serious air pollution here: 2,000 cars are added to the Kampala roads each month and the vast majority of them would not pass a basic safety assessment, let alone an MOT. Power and water cuts are as common as ever and there are ever increasing pressures placed upon the environment here. So, it is into this gloriously vibrant and chaotic city that we plunge each day, relying upon your prayers, His grace and our wits to get through the traffic with nerves, body and sanity intact. Much has happened since we last wrote to you all in January. There have been mountains to scale, valleys to traverse, as well as rainbows to surf...

Trip to South Africa

In March I was required to go to South Africa to do my annual South African Flight Exams. Appalling weather and a big red warning light (not a MAF plane!) as I landed my aircraft at East London meant that I got to spend the night in a 'motel' of note (and all the wrong notes, I hasten to add!) where the bed had one sheet and a pillow, both of which reeked of beer and smoke and were covered in a collection of stains I would rather not remember. So it was that I found myself in a rather insalubrious restaurant clutching my Coke (as in the drinking variety) whilst Nigerian drug dealers, guns included, dealt in a different type of coke. Being a pilot is exceedingly glamorous, as you can tell, and so I was very much into this role as I greeted the flight examiner in the same set of clothes the following day. That night Mike, on the other hand, found himself the proud owner of 2 hungry toddlers, and the absence of a toaster and bread meant that he couldn't cook for them. Thankfully, his inbuilt hunter-gatherer genes surfaced and he found a great ice-cream shop. He spent the remainder of the evening trying to peel them off the ceiling... A lot of our family reside in SA and so it was wonderful for them all to meet our children and for our children to meet them. It was so good to be around family again! It is very difficult being away from family and very hard to say goodbye at the airport, but it does make us more appreciative of them. I passed the exams, by the way.

In April Sam Tspawe (Jesus Film Ministry), Mike, the children and I all set off to Lira. We were on a 4-day trip back to this town that is situated around midpoint Uganda. Sam and I had been there a few months previously and wanted to re-visit the children of Lira Integrated School whom we had met on our first trip. This was one of the main reasons for this trip, as we both felt that we needed to see them again to see how they were doing and how best we could encourage them. It was to prove to be a challenging, encouraging and, at times, demoralizing 4 days. It was a privilege to spend time with the children, to share the Gospel with them, to pray with them, to let them talk. It was heart-breaking to see their physical and spiritual needs, to notice their lack of self-worth. Please pray for us as a family as we seek the Lord's guidance and timing, as we would like to re-visit the school and bring some basic health-care guidance, etc. On the Friday and Saturday we taught at a conference for leaders that had arrived from all over the area. It was a challenging trip in many ways and left us battling with an astounding selection of emotions as both Mike and I struggled to come to grips with much of what we had seen. Needless to say, our 2 children took it all in their stride and had a ball!

Caravan training

A special word of thanks to all of you who prayed for Mike and me these last 2 weeks as I undertook my Caravan training. Nope, not the kind you get stuck behind in Cornwall, but the type MAF flies. She has up to 14 seats and is much larger than the other 2 types of aircraft I fly. Mike spent many hours the week before we started going over various systems and trying to explain to me the various bits of the engine! To me it felt as if I was being asked to climb Mount Everest, and I approached the course with mixed feelings! Pickaxe and crampons to hand, I clung to Psalm 28v7: "The Lord is my strength and shield; my heart trusts in Him and I am helped; my heart leaps for joy and I will give thanks to Him in song." It never ceases to amaze me why God would call someone who cannot put a plug on the toaster without the help of *Reader's Digest* DIY manual to fly an aircraft with more knobs and buttons than the *Starship Enterprise*, but there you have it. What I can say is that, firstly, I have a wonderful husband who not only helped me prep for the event but also shouldered more of the childcare burden, and, secondly, that if God is calling you to the impossible, don't worry if you think that you cannot do it because, if you are like me, you cannot, but He can. Please do pray for Mike and me and the children, as I now fly much longer days and do a lot more cargo unloading, and so can be quite tired by the time I get home. Please do pray for my safety as I settle down to flying this new type of aircraft.

Riots

Thank you to all of you who prayed for us and for Uganda during the riots here last month. We are ever-mindful of the fact that things can, and do, quickly get out of hand. We were not even aware that demonstrations were planned for that day. Several of the MAF families had taken their children out, us included, to the same place. We had originally thought to go to a park in town right where the riots were, but all ended up going in the other direction. We were aware of how the Lord had shielded us that day. The riots ended up being racially motivated, being anti-Asian. One of the MAF staff members is part-Asian and this was very scary and hurtful to her and her daughters. Please do pray for peace here and for unity within our programme.

Lack of fuel

Over Easter we had a fuel shortage. Entebbe airport ran out of fuel! Several of the airlines had to route via Nairobi to refuel. We at MAF used our back-up stock. Praise God that we had enough to see us through the week-long shortage and that the people we fly were able to go where they needed to. We also had a severe diesel shortage that lasted around 5 weeks. We simply could not get fuel for our cars. It would arrive in dribs and drabs and we would mobile text message each other if we found any. Folk would then dash down to that particular station and wait in the long queue for a rationed amount of fuel.

Turkey

This week I read an article about 3 Christians in Turkey who were brutally tortured and then murdered for their faith by 5 Muslim youths whom they were reaching out to. I thought once again about the differences between these two faiths. The Muslim faith presents a god who offers 'heaven and paradise' to you if you die killing others; you gain your 'salvation' through a brutal and selfish one-off act. The Christian faith offers you salvation through a God who loves you so much that HE dies the brutal death and asks us to lay down our lives DAILY for others, not out of fear, but out of love. Islam is gaining deep inroads into Uganda. Please do pray for wisdom here as to how and when to reach out and show His love to the many Muslims who are seeking God and yet live in such terrible spiritual bondage. The ministry needs around us are simply overwhelming; please earnestly pray that we will do only the ministry that He asks us to and that we will have peace about it. I very much felt the Lord tell me that I cannot make a difference, only He can; all that I can do is the bit He asks me to. There are many times I fail miserably in my witness because I get frustrated or impatient, so please do pray for me as the Lord helps me deal with these weaknesses in my character.

Prayer and Praise

➢ Praise God for time with our family, a safe trip and successful exams.

➢ Praise God for our health and continued safety as we drive and fly.

➢ We thank God for all of you who are in this with us and who hold us in our times of weakness.

➢ Please pray for us as a family as we adjust to longer flying days.

➢ Please pray for our programme as pilots and engineers start going on furlough and so we have less staff to do the tasks.

➢ Please pray for wisdom, patience and a heart of love, especially during those times when we are beset by belligerent officials and mind-numbing bureaucracy.

➢ Please pray as we plan our furlough for this August.

Finally, I read this the other day and was most encouraged, so you may be too…

"May He make you so conscious of His indwelling…that you may realise…that in Him the weak is strong, the ignorant wise, the mute eloquent, the incompetent all-sufficient, and that in *Christ Jesus* there is no male or female, that so far as moved *by* Him, and acting *for* Him, you are no longer a girl whose place it is to keep back, retired and silent, but His instrument, called to adorn Him who is your adornment." Hudson Taylor of CIM, whilst in China to Jennie Faulding who 'ran' the CIM 'office' in London, 1871.

Dear Friends and Family: 10 June 2007

We have a mature, faithful little maroon beastie built by someone in Solihull well over a decade ago, and she proved her worth today. As previously mentioned, parts of the road system here are in the throes of refurbishment, the remainder in the throes of death. On our way home from church today we discovered what it is like to drive in a fast-flowing river! All the 'bits' were turned into red rivers as huge amounts of water rushed to the lowest points of Kampala. It was quite spectacular. We had no idea where the holes were and how deep they were. The dirt roads became swollen, mud rivers and the whole Land Rover misted up as the water poured in from the tops of the doors (a special design feature) so that we were forced into (gasp) wiping the INSIDE of the windscreen, a cardinal sin apparently. The windscreen wipers worked furiously on one side, a bright orange duster the other. Mounds of rubbish flowed by, drains choked up and the tethered goats stood by, miserably dripping. Mike got that glint in the eye that all Land Rover enthusiasts suffer from, as he diff-locked the car and tackled the free 4X4 course. Once again, thanks to all of you who pray for our safety!

On Tuesday I completed my first 'solo' Caravan flight. We do the extensive 2 weeks' training that MAF provides here, and then one has to do 25 hours of flying with a Supervisory Pilot, who checks that you are doing everything taught during training. That was all completed and so Tuesday found me on my own. I had a good flight into the Sudan. I flew up a team of 7 who were setting up and facilitating a week-long conference for pastors in Southern Sudan. Six of them were 40(plus)-something chaps from America. The seventh was a thin, unassuming Sudanese, called Paul Monyok. He is one of the 'Lost Boys' of Sudan. Around 20 years ago a group of boys fled the war in the Sudan and walked around 1,000 miles to Ethiopia! The USA accepted them all into their country. It was very interesting talking to Paul. He still lives in the States but does not have a very strong accent. He is just finishing theological training. It was his first time back in Sudan since he walked out during the war. I asked him how long it had been before he had been able to let his family know that he was still alive. He explained to me that, even once he had written to them, sent them a photo, etc., they still did not believe it. One of his sisters lives in Uganda and he met her last year - she just collapsed and cried. Once we had landed in Sudan he got chatting to his fellow countrymen in Sudanese and tried his hand at using a machete to cut the grass (he was somewhat 'rusty' and managed to hack up more dirt than trim grass, so we all had a good laugh!). I was so struck by how God works, how He redeems that which Satan means for our destruction! Sometimes the smallest acts of kindness have great outcomes. We may not even ever see these outcomes, but many others will reap the benefits.

Paul Monyok and group

On Wednesday I flew a family of four out of Gulu back to Kampala. They all live in the States, so parents were bringing their 2 children back to see Gulu; one had been born there. They were Mennonites and had been in Gulu 15 years ago. At that time they were the only *muzungus* in Gulu and one of the very, very few relief workers/missionaries there. Now there are many agencies in Gulu and numerous *muzungus*. I thought of how abundant the crop was from those little seeds that they had sown in faith, by His grace, all those years ago.

On Thursday I flew a group of 5 from Samaritan's Purse up to Arua. Arua is right on the Congolese border. 4 members of this group (2 couples) were well into their

70s and had been missionaries in the Congo many years before. They, plus a young Canadian lady, were returning to Adi in the Congo to set up house once again so that others could follow them! The young lady will be working as a nurse. I unloaded 321kg of freight for this venture. Sadly, we had to leave the double mattress at Entebbe as we were not able to get 10 people plus it into the cabin without blocking the exits!

Many thanks to you all for your continued prayers and for the work out here and worldwide that you all make possible. I certainly get to meet a lot of interesting people out here; we pray that we get to meet you all in August.

With much love,

Mike, D & I and Laura.

Dear friends and family...:
21 June 2007

Bumping along the road chatting away as I watch the children play, the green fields and hills juddering past, the sunbeams shining through the gaps in the cloud, I find that I have to remind myself I am in 'war zone' on standby. Most of the people I have just met, and most of those I am being driven past, have survived years of bloody war. Their smiles and quiet stares in no way reveal their terrors of the past, their nightmares of the present and their very real fears for the future. Here and there men stroll about in uniform, AK-47 slung over the shoulder. The airstrip I am on my way to has 3 large gun positions and a small group of soldiers camping at one end. Peace comes and goes. Rumours of failed peace talks and imminent faction-fighting abound. Yet, amidst all this, there is another kind of army; an army that has been growing quietly over the last 8 years; an army within an army.

I am driving from the FRM (Far Reaching Ministries) compound in Nimule, Sudan to the airstrip. The trip is slow going over the rough track.  We stop for cows to cross. There in the distance stands one of these special soldiers. He is guarding the aircraft. He is dressed in military fatigues, but what makes him different is the black cross 'flash' on his upper right arm. He is an army chaplain. This soldier is one of 50 who have just successfully completed a year's training with FRM at its Bible College down the road. He will join well over 140 other army chaplain soldiers already dispersed within the SPLA (Sudanese People's Liberation Army). Their mission: to spread the Gospel, to take the Good News to their fellow soldiers. At this time there are rumours of a 3-way split within the SPLA and of war. These men whom FRM has trained over the last 8 years have each chosen a demanding and personally risky career path. They have chosen to be soldiers in His army. Today I am flying Lindsay and Justin Holcomb, together with Mel Wilenson, back to Entebbe, Uganda. They have all been working at the FRM College, teaching and assisting as needed. The FRM compound also houses a Ladies' Sewing Course, from which 20 women have just graduated, and an extensive Sunday school programme which around 200 children attend each week. Vicky and Wes Bentley 'run' the operation here in Nimule as well as in Kitgum, Uganda. FRM is one of our partners (you will see its logo on one of the aircraft) here in Uganda. It has a huge outreach programme in Kitgum in early July, during which around 3,000 garments made by the ladies on the course in Nimule will be distributed and a 2-day Bible course run, amongst other things. Please do pray for the new chaplains, the 20 ladies who now return to their homes each with her own sewing machine, equipped to feed their families, the outreach programme in early July, and for Vicky and Wes as they lead the teams.

I was also so encouraged to fly a team of 5 young adults from Entebbe to Iquitos, Sudan. Alice, Andy, Dan, Heather and Scott are all working with African Inland Mission. They will be helping Josiah build relationships with the local folk in the area and do evangelism as well as build a new training facility. Josiah has been in Iquitos for 2 years now and was very excited to meet the team. Please pray for this team and for Josiah and his family as they serve in Sudan.

What made the day really special was that, on board, I had 2 MAF representatives who were able to *really* see what MAF does, who they serve and the impact these people are having in both Sudan and Uganda. Revd Glyn is a 'rep' in Essex and Martin is a 'rep' in Scotland. They return to the UK this week, so please pray for their trip back home.

Mike is quietly working on the next generation of MAF pilots…

Lord, I really love this job! I would have never known about these chaplains otherwise! How You laid this upon the hearts of Vicky and Wes and how they obediently acted upon hearing Your voice is wonderful. To know that in Sudan there are now hundreds of chaplains IN THE ARMY, all with the blessing of the Sudanese government, is mind-blowing! Lord, keep these chaplains strong, keep them safe, multiply their effectiveness as only You can. Let them be a sweet fragrance within Sudan, amidst the war and the poverty. Let them be Your voice of hope amidst hopelessness, Your hands of healing where there are no doctors, Your teachers where there is no education. Let them show how do love, how You promote justice and equality, how You promote peace and reconciliation.

Bless Vicky and Wes with ALL that they may need to continue in this ministry. May they continue to find favour with the government, with their supporters back home, with the people they train and with those they live among. Keep them healthy. I pray especially for Vicky, whose health is so precarious; shield her body from all infections and all harm. As she trusts in You, restore her strength daily so that she may run and not grow weary, walk and not grow faint, in accordance with Your promises.

For all the time Vicky and Wes have to spend apart, I pray that You protect their marriage and that You protect their love for each other. I pray that You give them time together and that You bless them with all good things. Amen.

CBM Flight: 27 June 2007

One of the organisations we at MAF fly on a regular basis is CBM (Christian Blind Mission). This Christian NGO has worked all over the world for many years now, seeking to help restore physical (and spiritual!) sight to the poor and underprivileged.

Dr Keith Waddle, a fantastic gentleman now into the autumn years of his life (ahem!) has been in Uganda since 1964. He has been working with CBM since 1982! I wonder how many eyes he has operated on in this time? How many people see as a result of the work he and his assistants do? I flew Dr Waddle and his 3 assistants out of Soroti and into Matany. They did around 70 operations last week whilst in Soroti, mostly on children. They are now spending a week in Matany (Karamajong area of Uganda) where they expect to do around 60-70 operations. As this area is very dry and consequently folk do not have spare water to wash their faces with, many people suffer from Trachoma. So, Dr Waddle explained to me that he will be mostly treating this, as well as operating on the very many cataract patients he will meet. MAF will pick him and his team up late next week and fly him to Kotido, where he will spend another week doing more operations. Thereafter, 4 days home and then off to the Congo! I just marvel at this man who hardly sees home and who has worked so tirelessly for so many years in Uganda and the surrounds. Thanks to all of you who support CBM and MAF!!!

Dr Keith Waddle and team

Lord, thank You for showing me such grace, such perseverance and such commitment to You in my meeting with Keith. Thank You for missionaries who spend all their lives serving You and spreading Your love where You have called them. In Keith I see one who is faithfully running the race, a long race. I see a man who gathers others around him as he runs, who not only runs for himself but who encourages others to run with him and who keeps them going. I see a man who looks past his own comfort, who, like Paul, has learnt to be content in all circumstances. Praise You, Lord, for this man! Praise You for all those he heals, for the sight he restores, for the lives he changes, all in Your name. Bless him in all he does. Amen.

A wet and wild week!
6 July 2007

It is rather hard to let you all know what happened over the last few weeks quite simply because I have been very busy flying (just about every day) and I can't really remember! What I can tell you is that we have had the most appalling weather! The lowest ever recorded temperatures (around 16°C is cold for the Equator), copious amounts of rain and persistent low cloud and thunderstorms.

I can tell you that I picked up the Samaritan's Purse team from Arua last week. Their trip to the Congo had been very successful and they managed to install the generator and solar systems into the hospital. It was the first time EVER that the hospital had had power! The team reported that, on the first day it was all in, over 15 operations were carried out for the first time under lights! They were thrilled to see the lights burning in the hospital late into the night.

On Monday we flew a large team from Far Reaching Ministries to Kitgum. Once again, the weather was terrible and both Simon and I had to work very hard to get them all there safely.

On Tuesday I flew a group up to Sudan. The new Operations Manager, Adrian Went, came along for the day. Well, it turned out to be quite an adventure! It was a day spent fighting the weather, with numerous diversions to other airfields and runways too waterlogged and muddy to land on. It seemed like an eternity before we headed back to Entebbe, only to find that the weather 50 miles from there was too severe to pass. It meant yet another diversion and a landing at a remote strip used by the oil concession companies! We spent the night in tents; the passengers were not thrilled, but were all very good-natured about it. We later learnt that 60000 people had been left homeless that day by flash floods in the Sudan and that an aircraft had crashed in Kenya that morning due to the bad weather. One passenger had just come out of hospital following a serious motorbike accident and another passenger had a baby which fell ill.

We tried for home the next day, only to encounter more severe weather which had me fly them all back to the remote strip. The passengers were put onto a bus and went to Entebbe, whilst Adrian and I got to spend another night camping. He worked hard clearing mud off the aircraft, whilst I got filthy refuelling the old girl.

On Thursday we finally got back to Kajjansi, Kampala. As we arrived, fog was rapidly moving in over the airfield; 15 minutes later and we would have had to go elsewhere.

Many thanks to you all for your prayers. God kept us safe and got each of us back in one piece. Mike and the children were ill the whole time with 'flu and fever! We praise and thank God for getting us through this very challenging time, and the family is slowly returning to full health.

Simon and I are the only two remaining pilots on the programme at this stage, and we are working very hard. Please do pray for us; that we will remain fresh, safe and healthy. Please also pray for our families, especially the spouses who are left at home with the children who are on school holidays!!!!

Lord, thank You for keeping us safe. Thank You for those who prayed for us today and for hearing their prayers! Thank You that I am not God and so I could entrust my medevac patients to Your care as we unexpectedly spent the night in tents, nowhere near the hospital they were supposed to be flying to. Thank You for the gap in the weather You gave so we could eventually get home.

I pray for Mike and the mums, who will soon have kiddies on hand 24/7. It is always hard to find things for them to do; please help those who are caring for their children these holidays. Let it be a fun time, let them all stay healthy, let them all enjoy being with each other.

Amen.

A rather mixed bag: 11 July 2007

Some days are more challenging or more interesting than others.

On Monday I started out the day by flying the American Ambassador and the MP for Bundibugyo (far-western Uganda) from Kampala to 'Bundi'. World Harvest Mission (WHM) has a base there. Drs Jennifer and Scott Myrehe and their colleagues run a medical outpost in this remote part of Uganda. They had just completed installing a midwifery wing at the hospital and the Ambassador was going to 'open' it. We landed at 'Bundi' to much fanfare, dancing and well-dressed WHM-ers!

Then it was off to Ishasha to pick up an archbishop, 3 bishops and 2 fathers! It was quite the 'purple' flight! I flew them all up to Yei, Sudan. Their mission: to encourage and build up their church colleagues in Sudan. The Sudanese church has seen years of persecution and suffered through several wars, and the country itself faces enormous challenges: drought, poverty, lack of infrastructure, etc.

The last leg of my day was quite different. A young man, on the back of a truck, had been thrown off during a road accident, and had broken his neck. I was medevacing him out, together with his wife and mother. He needed to get to Kampala International Hospital. His head had bolts in it, with a bag of sand hanging off these: a makeshift traction on his broken neck. The stretcher had wheels that wouldn't fold up, so it was a real challenge getting him into the back of the Caravan and strapping him down so that nothing moved during flight. It was late afternoon by now, with a fair bit of turbulence about. Apart from having your neck broken, then having to fly for the first time in your life, you then get turbulence! I wondered what would happen to him and his family. I thought, too, about the work of MSF ('medicine without frontiers') all over the world - it had arranged the medevac and given the man the best treatment in Gulu that it could.

I got home very late that night, exhausted and dirty, but I had my legs; yes, MAF makes a difference.

Lord, thank You so much for your grace and Your help today. So many important decisions to make throughout the day. I think especially for the man I medevaced out and I lift him before You now. Lord, You know his needs, You know his great distress and his desire to be well. Please let Your healing hand touch him and restore him to wholeness. Strengthen his family as they face a future where they are no longer certain he will be able to support and provide for them. A wife whose heart is hurting, a mother whose heart is hurting. Help them know You are near and that You care. Thank You for the hearts of those in MSF who were moved to compassion and who helped him. Thank You for all those who support MAF to make this trip even a possibility. In Jesus' name, Amen.

Mildmay in Gulu: 6 September 2007

We have just had a group of MAF 'reps' visit us. Nicky, one of the 'reps', came with me to Gulu. It is a short flight, just over 1 hour. The drive would take around 7 hours. This time saving means that a group of Ugandan medical and administrative volunteers are able to do DAY medical 'safaris' to IDP camps in Gulu. Mildmay targets babies, children and mothers on these trips. MAF flies them up around every second Saturday.

The camp we visited was around 45 minutes away by car. 14 of us, together with 3 armed soldiers, squeezed into and onto the back of a small pick-up truck. It was a case of holding on for dear life as we bounced our way to Awi camp.

The group sets up a triage area. Folk are assessed and then sent off to the doctor, nurse or whoever. So it was that I spent the day in triage. My job: to weigh babies, children and mothers.

People waited for HOURS. When we left at 4pm there was still a long queue of people that had NOT been seen. The queue from the door to my 'post' took around 1 hour alone. A constant stream of ill children and babies filed past me. Many wore rags; some were simply half-dressed. None had shoes. I noticed how most of the people had very badly-damaged feet.

I saw many cases of malnourishment, skin infections, unhealed wounds, serious coughs and rashes.

What do you say when you weigh a 12-month-old baby and it is 6kg? I have a niece who is 6 months old and she weighs more than that. I was terrified that I would 'break' half the babies I picked up - they were more a collection of clothed twigs than babies. My daughter Deborah is just 4 and she weighs a solid 22kg: mostly muscle and attitude! I was stunned to find that most of the 7-8-year-olds weigh that! Most of the ladies I weighed were around 55kg.

When it was time to leave we simply had to go. I believe that MAF is highly privileged to fly this group of volunteers who go back to these camps month after month. They are all busy people and they told me that the only reason they can come is because they can fly and get there and back in a single day.

Lord, thank You for how you multiply the ministry people are called to. Our aircraft get them there safely and quickly, they are refreshed and relaxed. Their loved ones know that they will be high above the fighting below. You bring peace to them, to our passengers and to those they in turn bring Your Peace to. Amen.

6 September 2007

We are back in Uganda! It was a fantastic trip back home to the UK and we met up with a lot of fantastic folk. Thank you to all of you who came to see us and who loved us. Deborah and Ivan had a wonderful time, coping extremely well with the various hotel rooms and the 2,119 miles of driving. As always, it was a happy/sad experience leaving, but we are all glad to be back here in Kampala.

Deborah and Ivan were off to their new school Friday morning, mum just a tad emotional to see them trotting off with their new teachers, wearing their new uniforms.

On Monday I started flying again and visited a lot of places in Uganda. The rains here have simply not stopped, and vast areas of north-eastern Uganda are flooded.

On Tuesday I flew to Sudan. The weather was atrocious and I actually never made it to my intended destination, Nzara. I diverted to Yambio, an airstrip 10 miles away from where I wanted to be. 5 minutes after landing, the strip became a river as the heavens opened and we were all drenched through to the skin. I was due to take a medevac patient from Nzara; the poor man, a stroke victim, was driven in the back of a pick-up to Yambio. The 10 miles took one-and-a-half hours. He was semi-conscious. I got him onto the stretcher, strapped him in and we all waited and waited, and waited some more. Eventually it stopped raining and finally the runway was once again usable. Just then a group of Sudanese arrived; they had 2 badly-wounded men with them. Both had suffered head injuries in an accident. One had just come out of a coma. And so it was that MAF fulfilled its mandate of 'Flying for Life' as we flew 3 medevacs out of Sudan and to a hospital in Uganda.

The weather was terrible again yesterday (Wednesday), and some folk ended up not quite where they wanted to be in Uganda (ahem!), but I was able to get the precious blood supply I had on board into Moroto for the local hospital.

So, we are all settled in! Thanks to you all for your prayers; please keep praying for MAF, our family and our safety.

God bless you all, with love,

Laura.

18 September 2007

Rain, rain and more rain. It is as if the heavens partake in some vicious battle. Even those brief moments of sunshine, a temporary cessation of hostilities, find the skies scattered with low cloud, lazy foot-soldiers refusing to retreat. And, as in all wars, we find ourselves unwilling participants, attempting to move about as best we can. I do my best to safely manoeuvre my winged aluminium can between the towering mountains of climatic rage. An hour of buffeting and rain later, the passengers and I disembark at Gulu. The talk is of the flooding we have seen from the air. Rivers, exhausted, have given up and the water charges over their banks, invading fields and villages, washing away bridges, washing in malaria and dysentery. The drive to Bobi IDP camp takes 30 minutes. We, all squashed up on the back of a small pick-up, cling to her edges like a flock of demented parrots on a rubber perch in a Force 9 gale. But the road, as rough and pot-holed as it is, is a lifeline, a thin vein stretched out between the various camps, bringing in progress and news of peace. The vegetation drips contentedly, presenting the eye with a rich and brilliant Irish green. But the colour is the only similarity. Each blade of grass looks wild, is wild, shoving itself defiantly out of the red soil, one of a million spears stabbing the sky. Trees, aggressive with thorns, beautiful in bloom, house exotic birds and shredded plastic bags. A collection of 3 brick buildings marks the heart of the camp, the main building a bright, peeling blue. Dozens of attended plastic containers nestle up alongside the water pump, awaiting their turn to be filled. A large clearing, afforded shade by a modest yet lush tree, marks the centre. A goat, 3 small kittens and an assortment of hens (complete with chicks) form part of the waiting crowd. The Mildmay team unpacks and sets itself up for the day's work: triage beneath the tree, doctors in the 3 small rooms to the right, dispensary in the main hall to the left. Rows of patient mothers wait to have their children seen. Some are happy, chatting gaily. Others shuffle forward, an air of defeat hanging over them. One, kneading her breast in desperation as her baby sucks in vain for nourishment; the mother is pregnant, a toddler grappling with her skirt, an older daughter caring for a little son. They all look exhausted. Another mother: stretched-out skin on jutting bones, clutching a small replica of herself, her eyes distant and elsewhere. I help to take weights and temperatures. Two-and-a-half years of age; 12 kg. Pale skin - anaemia. Fine, straight, reddish hair - severe malnourishment. Rashes and fungal infections, coughs and runny noses. Open wounds and bruised hearts. The nurses quickly take down each patient's history and assess them, despatching them to the doctor, dispensary or pastor as appropriate. I walk the desperately ill ones to the front of the queue outside the doctor's door. Smiling children, crying children. Cheeky, twinkle-eyed children. Glazed-eyed children plagued by tormenting flies. Hungry children and thin children. Little hands and little feet, little hearts all looking up at adults who shape and order their world. The team treats 300 of these small human promises and then we pack up and go. There is a temporary truce and the sun shines brightly as we fly home. Each day we fly over these camps, bowls of misery and suffering, of abject poverty and despair, where dreams are dreamt and hopes determinedly bubble up in the unbroken. And each day we fly in hearts and heads that care, hands and feet that wrestle with powers and forces beyond their control to help bring reality to those dreams and fulfilment to the hopes. Just before we land back at Kajjansi, we fly over Jaja's home. It is a part of Mildmay and it is a haven. Visiting, I find a beautiful place with green lawns, freshly painted buildings, safe playgrounds and clean corridors. HIV+ children from 0 to 17 years of age come here to be loved and treated - for free. Harriet shows me around: this room for 0-5 years, these for those 6-17 years of age. She shows me little beds with little teddies that will be used by tired little bodies later on today. A wall of coloured paper stars, each bearing a name, a reminder of those who have lost their battle with HIV/AIDS. Harriet shares about how the new staff all go home with swollen eyes for the first few weeks; how each of them has to learn to mourn the little ones who they grow so attached to and who then perish. How they have to guard their hearts from becoming hard and yet not allow them to break; of the joy of seeing a child recover and respond to their love and their treatment. The children are picked up in the morning and taken home around 4pm, their daylight hours spent playing, laughing, sleeping and eating, as well as receiving medical care. In each room happy faces - children being children. Sister Margret shows me around their hospital -

30 beds, each a cocoon of loving care that holds an HIV+ child as he or she is either nursed back to health or released into the arms of the Good Shepherd.

I ponder greatness. It is attributed to those who lead countries or massive NGOs, who scale a mountain or cross the Atlantic in a bathtub. But here I see life, good and bad, two sides of a coin, simultaneously in the same, small space. And it is here that I see greatness in the Unknowns: the desperate mother who toils and fights to put a single meal on the family table, the father who carries his sick child for miles to a clinic, the sturdy hands of nuns that have spent 30-something years caring for those in need around them, the unassuming doctors and nurses in places like Mildmay Jaja's home who love and care for the dying. "Whoever welcomes this little child in my name welcomes me; and whoever welcomes me welcomes the one who sent me. For he who is least among you all – he is the greatest." Luke 9v48.

News from Mike and Laura: October 2007

Dear friends and family

Last month saw the second anniversary of our being here in Uganda. Wow! How time has whizzed by! We would have to say that these past 2 years have been very interesting, very challenging and very blessed. We also would want to say that they could not have been done without all of you: the faithful prayers, cares and giving that have made it possible for us to be here doing what we are doing.

June and July flew past, quite literally. It felt as if I spent more time in the air than on the ground, dodging huge thunderstorms and long walls of impenetrable rain whilst Mike sent weather updates over the cell phone system. On a few occasions I never made it home, 'camping' it out in some obscure part of Uganda with a group of mildly disgruntled passengers who joined me in scouring the skies for the faintest glimmer of blue.

August was a great month! We all flew back home to the UK for a 4-week furlough and got to meet a lot of you, visit Tesco and enjoy 24/7 hot water and electricity! A massive 'Thank You' to all of you who came to see us and hear what God is doing in Sudan and Uganda. We went home to Uganda greatly encouraged with our energy and enthusiasm renewed. Deborah and Ivan went with us to a re-enactors' event in Maidstone and got their first lesson in UK history, cannons and all!

We got back to Uganda and started looking for someone called Noah who was building a boat... In all seriousness, the rains that had been a blessing continued unabated and we found ourselves dealing with floods. The last bridge north collapsed last week, making it 26 bridges unusable and most of the north cut off. It is strange flying over trees that look like they are ice-skating. I look down to see little green patchwork quilts drowned beneath a watery blanket, little specks that turn out to be great trucks halted in their tracks by a missing bridge, swollen green arms that turn out to be a new tributary of the Nile. MAF is working to meet the needs; Simon Wunderlii flew around 2000 kg of freight up to Morulem on Saturday and Adrian Went and his team in operations have been frantically working to juggle all the flight requests.

In September Wayne and Bev Stevens of Cornerstone Foundation (Australia) arrived in Uganda. This couple is one of MAF's customers and we have had the privilege of flying them to Kitgum over the years. It has been a real struggle for them: they have 2 containers full of equipment on a boat anchored somewhere off Mombasa! As the roads are flooded none of the containers can be sent out, which means no new ones can be off-loaded! Once they do get off-loaded it will be a while before they reach Kampala and even longer before they can reach Kitgum in the far north of Uganda. Wayne and Bev are living with us in the interim and have become impromptu grandparents to Deborah and Ivan! They are here to build and open a vocational training centre for teenage boys and girls who need love, care and a chance to make something of their lives in an area blighted by war and poverty. Mike is very much involved in this project. Simply knowing Kampala as well as he does has proved to be a real blessing, as he and Wayne set off in the trusty old Land Rover in search of some or other obscure governmental department where a man with 'the stamp' is to be found. The two of them have become something of Knights of the Round Table in search of the Holy Grail, a Grail that consists largely of a phantom form at the end of a very long paper-chase.

In September I nipped back over to the UK to speak at an event in Sywell. A group of folk had come to hear about the work of MAF; for some it was their first introduction to MAF. There were many others present who had spent many years faithfully supporting MAF and it was a real treat for me to get to meet with many of them. We all got to hear Stuart King, one of MAF's founders, speak about the 'old days' in Sudan and he was fantastic. It is strange to think that these people are still at war all these years later. As I write, the situation grows more tense; parts of the unified government have boycotted government meetings and troops from both sides are steadily building in numbers in the oil-rich areas. I noted tinsel and Santa, along with mince pies, had made their way into the supermarkets already so I thought it would be OK to ask you all to pray for a season of goodwill for Sudan.

Here are some other areas we would ask you to pray about…

PRAISE

❖ A wonderful furlough with time for being with friends and family.

❖ Deborah and Ivan settling in well to 'big' school this September.

❖ Safe flying through a prolonged spell of atrocious weather.

❖ Good health for us all, the cat and the car.

❖ Safe trips in the car; 6 people die in road accidents in Kampala each day.

PETITION

❖ Peace in Sudan.

❖ Help for those affected by the floods.

- ❖ Wisdom for the MAF team in dealing with the floods, etc.

- ❖ The work of MAF during CHOGM when Her Majesty visits late November.

- ❖ Cornerstone Foundation couple, Wayne and Bev, as they wait and work towards the setting up of the training centre in Kitgum.

- ❖ Mike as he helps Wayne and Bev out in Kitgum and Kampala.

- ❖ God's guidance and peace as we look at what He has planned for us in 2008.

I have written quite a few emails which many of you would not have received, so I am including one of these. Please do let me know if you would like to be added to our email list. laura.westley@maf-europe.org should do the trick. Mike, Deborah, Ivan and I would love to wish you all a really blessed Christmas. We hope and pray that you all get to spend time with those you love. May God grant each of you His blessings and His peace during 2008.

With much love, Mike, Deborah, Ivan and Laura.

"We wait upon the Lord; he is our help and our shield. In him our hearts rejoice, for we trust in his name. May your unfailing love rest upon us, O Lord, even as we put our hope in you." Psalm 33v20-22

Rain and Gulu

Rain, rain and more rain. It is as if the heavens partake in some vicious battle. Even those brief moments of sunshine, a temporary cessation of hostilities, find the skies scattered with low cloud, lazy foot-soldiers refusing to retreat. And, as in all wars, we find ourselves unwilling participants, attempting to move about as best we can. I do my best to safely manoeuvre my winged aluminium can between the towering mountains of climatic rage. An hour of buffeting and rain later the passengers and I disembark at Gulu. The talk is of the flooding we have seen from the air. Rivers, exhausted, have given up and the water charges over their banks, invading fields and villages, washing away bridges, washing in malaria and dysentery. The drive to Bobi IDP camp takes 30 minutes. We, all squashed up on the back of a small pick-up, cling to her edges like a flock of demented parrots on a rubber perch in a Force 9 gale. But the road, as rough and pot-holed as it is, is a lifeline, a thin vein stretched out between the various camps, bringing in progress and news of peace. The vegetation drips contentedly, presenting the eye with a rich and brilliant Irish green. But the colour is the only similarity. Each blade of grass looks wild, is wild, shoving itself defiantly out of the red soil, one of a million spears stabbing the sky. Trees, aggressive with thorns, beautiful in bloom, house exotic birds and shredded plastic bags. A collection of 3 brick buildings marks the heart of the camp, the main building a bright, peeling blue.

Dozens of attended plastic containers nestle up alongside the water pump, awaiting their turn to be filled. A large clearing, afforded shade by a modest yet lush tree, marks the centre. A goat, 3 small kittens and an assortment of hens (complete with chicks) form part of the waiting crowd. The Mildmay team unpacks and sets itself up for the day's work: triage beneath the tree, doctors in the 3 small rooms to the right, dispensary in the main hall to the left. Rows of patient mothers wait to have their children seen. Some are happy, chatting gaily. Others shuffle forward, an air of defeat hanging over them. One, kneading her breast in desperation as her baby sucks in vain for nourishment; the mother is pregnant, a toddler grappling with her skirt, an older daughter caring for a little son. They all look exhausted.

Another mother: stretched-out skin on jutting bones, clutching a small replica of herself, her eyes distant and elsewhere. I help to take weights and temperatures. Two-and-a-half years of age; 12 kg. Pale skin - anaemia. Fine, straight, reddish hair- severe malnourishment. Rashes and fungal infections, coughs and runny noses. Open wounds and bruised hearts. The nurses quickly take down each patient's history and assess them, despatching them to the doctor, dispensary or pastor as appropriate. I walk the desperately ill ones to the front of the queue outside the doctor's door. Smiling children, crying children. Cheeky, twinkle-eyed children. Glazed-eyed children plagued by tormenting flies. Hungry children and thin children. Little hands and little feet, little hearts all looking up at adults who shape and order their world. The team treats 300 of these small human promises and then we pack up and go. There is a temporary truce and the sun shines brightly as we fly home. Each day we fly over these camps, bowls of misery and suffering, of abject poverty and despair, where dreams are dreamt and hopes determinedly bubble up in the unbroken. And each day we fly in hearts and heads that care, hands and feet that wrestle with powers and forces beyond their control to help bring reality to those dreams and fulfilment to the hopes. Just before we land back at Kajjansi, we fly over Jaja's home. It is a part of Mildmay and it is a haven. Visiting, I find a beautiful place with green lawns, freshly painted buildings, safe playgrounds and clean corridors. HIV+ children from 0-17 years of age come here to be loved and treated - for free. Harriet shows me around: this room for 0-5 years, these for those 6-17 years of age. She shows me little beds with little teddies that will be used by tired little

bodies later on today. A wall of coloured paper stars, each bearing a name, a reminder of those who have lost their battle with HIV/AIDS. Harriet shares about how the new staff all go home with swollen eyes for the first few weeks; how each of them has to learn to mourn the little ones who they grow so attached to and who then perish. How they have to guard their hearts from becoming hard and yet not allow them to break; of the joy of seeing a child recover and respond to their love and their treatment. The children are picked up in the morning and taken home around 4pm; their daylight hours spent playing, laughing, sleeping and eating as well as receiving medical care. In each room happy faces - children being children.

Sister Margret shows me around their hospital - 30 beds, each a cocoon of loving care that holds an HIV+ child as he or she is either nursed back to health or released into the arms of the Good Shepherd.

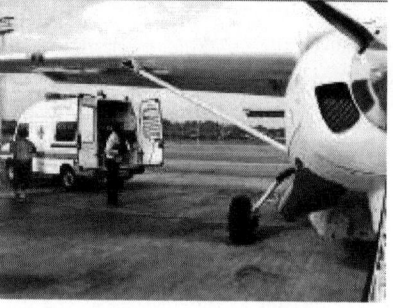

I ponder greatness. It is attributed to those who lead countries or massive NGOs, who scale a mountain or cross the Atlantic in a bathtub. But here I see life, good and bad, two sides of a coin, simultaneously in the same small space. And it is here that I see greatness in the Unknowns: the desperate mother who toils and fights to put a single meal on the family table, the father who carries his sick child for miles to a clinic, the sturdy hands of nuns that have spent 30-something years caring for those in need around them, the unassuming doctors and nurses in places like Mildmay Jaja's home who love and care for the dying. "Whoever welcomes this little child in my name welcomes me; and whoever welcomes me welcomes the one who sent me. For he who is least among you all – he is the greatest." Luke 9

Christmas Blessings

Love, peace and joy at Christmas and His blessings through 2008. Mike, Laura, Deborah & Ivan

Lord, thank You for these last 2 years in Uganda. I cannot always comprehend what I have seen, a lot I cannot ever forget. You have shown me what suffering en-masse is really like, how folk are stripped of their dignity, of hope, of a decent life. There is such misery, so much darkness; thank You for Your light, for the real hope You bring to countless people here in Uganda and Sudan. You have shown me how real Your Church is; how she is a home and a safe place for so many who have neither a home nor a safe place, how she works as Your hands and feet, how her heart reflects Your heart. You have shown me how each person has a part to play - their own, unique role. I think of those who support us here, those who faithfully pray and give, those who send emails and letters and Christmas cards. Lord, let them know the value of their part and bless them for what they help achieve in Your name. Amen.

Friday 19ᵗʰ

We had a staff 'quiet day'. These are held around every 3 months and we all take time out to be with each other, praise, and worship and reconnect with each other and with God. It was also an opportunity for Jacqueline Went to introduce the puppets that she brought over from the UK; Mike has got involved in this puppet ministry and so we got to see him (or his puppet at least) in action. Many folk had never seen anything like it before and it went down ever so well.

Puppet ministry; Mike in pink striped top!

This time I arranged for 3 of our 'customers' to come and speak about the work that they are doing here in Uganda and the Sudan.

Wayne and Bev, Cornerstone Foundation Australia, spoke to us about their vision for a training centre in Kitgum and how that project is taking place slowly but surely. They have been raising the funds in Australia, and obtaining the necessary equipment, for over 7 years. For some of our Ugandan staff it was the first time that they had seen footage of LRA victims in the north. It was a reminder to all of us of why we are here.

Steve (our boss) and Shelly, Medair

Shelley of Medair came and spoke to us about the work of Medair in the north east of Uganda. They have several projects on the go. One of them is up in the Kaabong area where they are working to help people fix and clean their water supplies. Most of the water people drink is contaminated, so getting clean water will mean an end to numerous health problems. Medair aims to train local folk to be self-sustaining once the team leaves the area. Another project is about bringing basic health care to the

IDP camps; their vision is to simply improve the life of those in the IDP camps, a really tall order!

Margret and Roger came over from Mildmay Jaja's home and spoke to us about the work that they are doing in both Kampala and Gulu. They run HIV/AIDS clinics, hospitals, training courses, etc. Jaja's home deals with HIV+ children. It was wonderful to see the before-and-after photos of children in both Gulu's IDP camps as well as in the home in Kampala; the children were alive and well, having been brought in on the brink of death. It was so encouraging to all of us, especially those whose work is in the office or in finance or the maintenance yard, where the end result of their labours is not at all obvious.

It was so good to be able to see how flying aircraft helps others to reach those so desperately in need, and also to remind folk that whatever part they 'play' in MAF, it is a team effort and we really cannot do without each other.

We had some friends over for dinner and later I went out to help with the church youth group. We are talking about relationships between boys and girls (!) The ladies were talking about modesty and the chaps were talking about how they view women; as objects or as people. The evening started off eventfully when a local *mutatu* (minibus) driver almost knocked one of the young lads down on the road outside the place we were meeting. A group of Ugandan thugs got out and basically demanded that the youth, a lad of around 15, pay for the broken window; broken as the driver had hit the lad who was walking on the side of the road!!! It is so disheartening at times to be in a country, trying to help, where just about everyone is trying to get your money; you are foreign so you must be rich, so I deserve some of your money! Drives me nuts!

Saturday 20th.

I flew a lady into Sudan. She heads-up the Far Reaching Ministries team there. They are planning a ladies' conference next weekend. Vicky lives mostly there, she loves the place! We chatted (well, given the ambient noise level in a Cessna 210, shouted!) the entire 2 hours!

Mike helped Wayne tinker on the Land Rover; they all came out to Kajjansi to meet me when I landed; what a good sight to see! We then all headed off into the messy traffic to get some shopping done. Took us an hour to travel around 15km.

Sunday 21st.

Last night's thunderstorm was special! The thunder woke Mike and Steve up; Bev, the children and I all slept through!

Church was great and we had another challenging yet building sermon. Got to meet some new folk and have a coffee. Deborah and Ivan came out of Sunday School with lovely paintings that said: "Jesus is my sunshine", so I pinned them onto the fridge (the paintings, not the kids!) Our church is on Gaba Road, one of the routes dignitaries will use during CHOGM. There is a good chance it will be closed at a moment's notice, so we are thinking of doing church in various people's homes that Sunday.

Monday 22nd

Last night's thunderstorm woke even Bev and me up! Set the entire neighbourhood's dogs off howling and all car alarms!

Rearranged our flights this morning so that we could fit in a Medevac (someone in Gulu had a serious compound fracture and was laid-up on a stretcher somewhere); Simon did the western side of Uganda and I the east. Very turbulent today, so quite a few folk got sick. I am told that as a result of the floods Soroti, which I flew over, has been overrun with snakes and crocodiles. Made me look extra hard at the gauges; don't want to be doing any forced landing around there, thank you very much!

Mountains = turbulence!

Mike went out for the evening; he does 'puppet ministry' on Mondays. They look like the Muppet puppets; he missed his calling in life as he should have been a stand-up comedian, he is just sooo funny! I so wish I was a fly on the wall, as what he recounts sounds quite hysterical! They practise very hard. You are only able to move your thumb and you have to have your arm pointing straight up for the entire 5-minute song, so he had cramp to start with but has grown accustomed to it now.

Mike also took Wayne to the doctor. Wayne has an ulcer! They spent hours waiting for the doctor to arrive and do the endoscopy; he was running late. Not by a few minutes; try two-and-a-half hours. Anyhow, then they had to wait for around an hour to get the results. It took 90 minutes to drive the 10km home.

Tuesday 23rd

Flew 2 chaps from the EU up to Moroto today. They almost missed their flight as at 0900hrs they were in the bank in town instead of at the airport! Time in Africa can mean very little... They are going there to train folk in how to go about applying for EU development grants. They told me that they make sure the money is spent as it was applied for and that the money goes to helping provide sources of fresh, safe drinking water, maintaining school and hospital buildings, etc. Once again it was a very turbulent day. After I had shut down the aircraft, one chap insisted on praying for me as I flew back! An unexpected blessing!

A truck got stuck on the narrow road outside the airport that we use to get home so, after waiting around 20 minutes, we did a u-turn and had to take the 4x4 'off road'. All very exciting! The place is mad with road-works, and posters asking "Are you ready for CHOGM?"

Praying passengers!

Had some friends over for dinner prior to the prayer meeting which was held at our place tonight. Lots to pray about. The local CAA finally granted our annual AOC (Air Operator's Certificate) so that was a praise item! A friend of one family was kidnapped in Chad 2 weeks ago and no one has heard a thing; a church in a remote part of Madagascar has come under serious attack and people there resistant to the Gospel had threatened to shoot the MAF aircraft down, so it was unable to land there; a friend from Congo has just been operated on for suspected bladder cancer; etc. We all shared tea, biscuits (from a packet!) and cake (baked by me and only slightly burnt on the bottom!) and nattered for an hour before folk went home. I am flying tomorrow so it was straight to bed.

Wednesday 24th

Wayne up all night with the ulcer. Mike carted him back off to the doctor. The medication is working in part but, if it does not improve, he will need something a little more serious. I try to tip-toe about at 0530hrs so as not to wake the household, but the cat hears me and meows at the door to be let in. She is VERY persistent and has me well-trained so I let her in. She caught a mouse the other day, so has her uses... I think that Wayne would like to own a fur hat...

I did the milk run again today, carting folk all over Uganda. We routed Amudat (around one-and-a-half hours away) then Moroto then Kotido then Kaabong then Gulu then Lira and, finally, back to Kajjansi. It is very much like a bus service! It was incredibly turbulent today so many of the poor passengers got ill. Always feel so bad when that happens as they are hardly in a position to work and the nearest cup of tea is a long way away.

After landing I went back to the office to join in the pilots' meeting; we were there until 5pm, going over various operational issues. The big question is: are we ready for CHOGM?!!!

Mike and I decided to pop out for ice-cream once the children had gone to bed (having Wayne and Bev to stay is great!) It used to be a great place; you bought a paper cup of Italian-style ice-cream from inside the 'supermarket'. Sadly, this section has been moved to a nearby 'shelter' of dubious hygiene standards. We braved it; wooden benches with dirty, plastic-covered tables. I had a view of a mange-infested cactus and Mike got the dustbin. A rather large and elongated dropping decorated the table, so I decided to hold on to the cup… Anyhow, it turns out the ice-cream tasted 'dodgy'. Must have melted, or not been frozen at the right temperature. Who knows? Anyhow, dysentery in mind, we decided to give it a miss and not revisit.

Thursday 25th

As usual, at the office at 0630hrs for the day's flying schedule. The customer apparently wanted only to leave at 0930hrs instead of 0800hrs so I went home for a coffee and to see the kids wake up. Left a short while later, only to find that the 4 passengers had been at the airfield since 0730hrs! Their boss had told them to get there for 0730hrs! It was a group of 4 working for AMREF; they were flying to Soroti to audit the hospitals that they are providing medicine to. Profuse apologies and we were off. I will pick them up tomorrow.

There is a flying school at Soroti and so I got surrounded by eager young and budding aviators who all wanted to look inside the Caravan. It is always a thrill to meet those starting out on their flying careers as they are enthusiastic and excited about the whole thing!

Igor and Igor of the Ukraine

Met Igor and Igor, two Ukrainians who were bashing some or other bit of a Mil-8 helicopter. They are flying for the UN, dropping food into the flooded areas of Uganda. They go to Sudan next. It must be really hard for them, as they speak only the most limited amount of English (I speak limited Russian and am good at hand signs...) and work in all the tough spots of the globe. Very few are Christians, so I hope they eventually figure out what MAF is and does and that somehow they are witnessed to, and so get to meet, Jesus. Then flew to Lira where I picked up Sam (Jesus Film Ministry) and 10 of his colleagues. They have all spent a few days ministering to folk in Lira. I asked how it went and he said: "Brilliantly"! For most of the pastors this mission has given them their very first opportunity to fly.

I have been doing a lot of work on a course for Entebbe Air Traffic Control over the last few weeks. I will run the course on Tuesday, Wednesday and Thursday next week. The course deals with helping controllers to be trained to deal with unusual and emergency situations. Who would have ever thought that I would do that in Uganda? Anyhow, met up with the local charter company after my flight today, to get their input on various issues. I pray that the course goes well as it will certainly bring added safety to all the pilots flying in Uganda.

Home by 6pm and was greeted enthusiastically by Mike and the kids! Mike was back to the doctor with Wayne this morning. He has also figured out Skype and so went off into the market to find a headset! It was 3GBP. Amazing what you can find there. Wayne has to find some extra pillows, which one has to be careful with as you never know what has got INTO the pillow, so you have to buy one in a sealed bag and so it costs a fair whack. Still, better than bed lice or something even more exotic!

Friday 26th.

Had some really encouraging news in today! I flew up a group of folk from Church of Christ, USA to Nimule, Sudan, last week. They had brought hundreds of pairs of spectacles. I took them up on Tuesday and they flew back on Thursday; on each day they managed to see around 200 folk, testing their eyesight and giving out glasses to those in need. For most of these people, this will be the only time they will ever see an optician! Talk about bringing sight to the blind!

Mike and Wayne spent most of the day in town, chasing various 'stamps' required on paperwork; Wayne is attempting to obtain a tax number. The tax office told him to get it in Kitgum; he pointed out that the roads to Kitgum were all closed due to the flooding. It has taken around 8 trips, many hours of waiting and even more of frustration, but hopefully he will be issued with a tax number on Monday next week.

I flew up to Morulem and Moroto. I took a Japanese doctor into Morulem. He has taken a year out from his work in Japan to help out in hospitals in Uganda. He has left his family behind and is now 11 months in to his 12-month stay. What is truly remarkable is that the doctor is disabled due to childhood polio, and there is NO provision for the disabled in Uganda. One of the other passengers was a well weathered nun off to Moroto; 26 years of service to the Karamajong continuing unabated. Another was a young man from New York City who works for Rescue International. We all spent several hours bouncing around the mountains like a cork in a thunderstorm, trying not to be ill! The afternoon I spent putting the finishing touches to the ATC Emergency Training Course I will run at Entebbe next week. It was good to get home, albeit rather late. Mike was pleased to see me; it's been a tough week for him as the kids have been on half-term holidays!

Our local garage...

Kampala life

News from Mike and Laura December 2007

Saturday 24 November 2007

Take one old Land Rover, one old codger (sorry, Wayne) and one 6'7" hunk (that would be my hubby), play the *Mission Impossible* theme tune; watch them head off into the sunrise (not something that either of these chaps are accustomed to!!!) and then go back to bed!!! Wayne Stevens from Cornerstone Foundation, one of MAF's mission partners, and Mike were off to Kitgum.

Kitgum is on the northern border of Uganda, around 400km/250miles. Kitgum has an airstrip but is has become too unsafe to use as the local folk insist on using it as a road, a playground and grazing land. No amount of careful negotiations has been able to resolve this safety issue and so now folk have to drive in. What would have been a 90-minute flight became a twelve-and-a-halfhour drive! Each way. The journey was mechanically uneventful, apart from one flat tyre. Physically, it was a challenge! Constant 100% attention was required due to the numerous cavernous potholes, mud pools, crazy drivers and stray cattle. A large part of the drive was undertaken along the side of the road as it was more usable than the road itself. The recent flooding hadn't helped one bit and stranded trucks littered the roadside, an ugly string of broken beads marring an otherwise pretty countryside. They arrived at sunset, exhausted and thoroughly bone-rattled. It was the start of 2 weeks of cabbage, digestive biscuits, coke, dust and frustration. It is hard to explain the challenges of setting up a mission in Uganda. People, moved to compassion by the horrors of what the LRA have done, called by God, up sticks and come. They spend hours in prayer, years in planning and fundraising and arrive full of enthusiasm.

At this point, Satan moves into overdrive. Government departments, wary of NGOs due to the abuses and dishonesties of some in the past, don't make it any easier. Desperate people see you as a ticket out of their poverty-stricken situation, befriending you merely for what you can give, unaware and in disbelief that your supply of money is not yours and that it IS limited. Just about any 'service' provider you approach says one thing and provides another, both the cost and the actual product different on the day it arrives from the day it was ordered, never in your favour. It took the chaps days to arrange for cement, days to arrange for the gravel needed to mix with it, complex negotiations to obtain the water needed to make the cement, days to find men skilled enough to help mix it. All that Wayne and Mike had to do was lay 5 blocks of concrete of around 3m x 1m and get the local RDC (Regional Director) to sign their annual NGO renewal application. It took 2 weeks to lay 5 small blocks of concrete. Mike and Wayne worked long hours setting reinforcing wires, topping-off the cement blocks, etc. All at around 40°C! The RDC had given them an appointment for their penultimate day in Kitgum. They arrived at the appointed time, only to find that both he and the second in command were away on a course somewhere and would not be available for the next 5 days. It was vital that the paperwork was signed as their NGO certificate had expired.

Frustration upon frustration beset them. On returning to Kampala, Wayne discovered that the shipping company had still not managed to calculate the import taxes; this was 12 weeks after they were given the paperwork! The truck he hired to move supplies from one place to another on a given day was in Jinja, the Land Rover conked out, both he and Bev have the 'trots'... As an MAF pilot I see quite a bit of this; people eager to help thwarted at every turn. It is difficult to accept that, despite the obvious needs of the poorest of the poor, the desperation of so many children, teens, women and men, the powers-that-be do not always embrace or welcome an 'outsider's' help. People may ask me: "Do you think that there is a country that would actually want this help?" After the umpteenth disappointment, someone will say to them: "Ah, but it's all in God's timing" at which point an overwhelming desire to throttle them falls upon you! One knows that God has His timing. One also knows that He promised that this life would be a challenge. Knowing these things does NOT always make it easy to deal with the realities of constant disappointments, crushed hopes, people letting you down, lying to you, using you and then moving on to the next person. My heart really goes out to these missionaries; they often work against all the odds. Please do keep on praying for those we fly (and for those we cannot fly!) as they so need all the encouragement and strength that holding them in prayer gives.

Saturday 1 December 2007

What to make of Mongolia? Once I had gotten over the shock of being mugged by a polar bear for my jacket...; it's COLD! Around -26°C whilst we were there.

Less than 1% Christian, mostly Buddhist and Shamanic, temples and shrines dotted all over the place. An epic trip of 3 days to reach her, a Cyrillic alphabet, Oriental language and a bold attempt to forge her own future with a headlong plunge into Capitalism (both good and bad) following a release from her Communist past. Young adults and teenagers, impeccably dressed, enjoy what their parents never had. Sadly, there is high unemployment and many leave in search of a brighter future in Korea, Japan, or America.

We did a fair bit of on-foot exploring, really walking the length and breadth of Ulaanbaatar. It was an interesting kaleidoscope of life; a rich city centre with ancient Buddhist monasteries alongside brand new glass high rise buildings. Moving out just a fraction the older Soviet style buildings, Soviet regalia intact, ditto the mental approach to customer care and freedom of movement. At the fringes, the poorest of the poor. Battered gers on soil, each surrounded by its own fence and collection of mangy dogs, fleas long-frozen.

The folk here are so poor that they can afford neither coal nor wood and so they burn horse manure, litter, and plastic bags -whatever they can find.

The children do not have warm clothes as their folk cannot afford it, so they spend most of the winter (a mere 6 months) inside the ger, their legs buckling under them as they fail to grow normally and suffer from rickets.

MAF operates here as 'Blue Sky Aviation', traversing the length and breadth of the country on behalf of a wide selection of customers. Secular customers, such as medevacs for folk from the mining companies, are commercially charged so as to subsidise very heavily the work of Christian mission workers. Four-and-a-half hours' flying takes you to the far west at -40°C in the winter and at +40°C in the summer! Mike and I were both very at peace being here; we have prayed long and hard over the move and want to help and support the work of the Church as she grows here in Mongolia. We both feel that God could well be calling us here and have started working on the various bits we will need to complete to make this a reality. There are many mountains and challenges to overcome before we move to Mongolia. But just to give you a flavour of the place...

It was about 5pm, the sun sitting low on the horizon, when the ger became our home for the evening. A ger is a small, circular type of dwelling made up from a frame of wooden poles and covered in felt made from camel or yak fur. The door, the only opening bar a small opening at the apex that allows smoke to escape, was painted cherry red with intricate swirled patterns, a bright and vibrant greeting that invited you to leave the barren wilderness outside. Layers of clothing and boots, protection from the bone-snapping cold, are quickly abandoned as you enter into this haven of warmth. The door faces south so as to snatch each ray of sunshine this harsh winter begrudgingly parts with. Most folk bend to enter through the low door; Mike almost has to crawl, a collection of half-frozen legs and bright blue, padded jacket that covers everything apart from his eyes and nose.

At the centre of this circular house is a fire. Ours is an ancient iron affair that rapidly consumes wood and coal with extreme efficiency. You are sweating in minutes! Except for your feet which, as hot air rises, are too low down and remain ice-cold! Quite bizarre!

As the sun finally sets the cold draws in around the ger like a noose, quickly finding any gap and shooting icy fingers through it. Post-dinner, bed seems a wonderful place to be. Lights out, dancing phantoms frolicking across the walls courtesy of the burning embers, we settle down with our own small thoughts as the wind and the wolves howl to each other outside.

I awoke at 3am, quite frozen. The fire had gone out. I felt like I was in the freezer; I didn't want to move! I gazed up through the hole in the roof. Our earth turns with a beautiful precision. A new set of stars hung above me, shining white pearls on the smoothest of velvet black skies. Fire relit, we tossed and turned, fighting the cold until the morning returned. Showering was an exceedingly brief and frigid affair which deftly ensured that all traces of snooze were dismissed and that I was 100% awake.

The drive back to Ulaanbaatar took around 2 hours. 2 hours of vastness, of emptiness, of huge open spaces; of ice and mountains and shrines and horses. And not a yak in sight…

Saturday 8 December 2007

It's wonderfully pleasant, bouncing along as a passenger on the back of a bicycle-taxi, boots sticking out so as to keep clear of the chain. I have filed the flight plans for the rest of the day's flying, checked over the aircraft post-flight, chatted to the students at the flight school and in Air Traffic Control and secured my little winged friend against the dangers of sudden thunderstorms et al. Above, a clear blue sky with the promise of cooling cloud approaching from the east. The bell lets out a happy little tinkle as we jolt over each bump, and there is the soft whisper of air past my ears. There are not that many cars in Soroti, just those belonging to the better-established NGOs, so I am not too nervous a passenger today.

We cycle down the airport road and then left into the main street, both lined by well-spaced and gently decaying buildings of the 1950s in a sort of art deco style. The homes stand quietly, tatty tombstones draped in washing and surrounded by junk, to a past of only 50-60 years ago.

In the town centre a few have been repainted in bright colours, advertising *Telcom*, *MTM* and other mobile phone companies, bright beacons of hope to the promise of a country's resurrection from the miseries of war, flood and poverty.

My taxi drops me off at the Soroti Hotel. It is a neat and clean collection of low buildings, groomed gardens and a tatty back yard. The staff, watching CNN News and SkySport football on the various TVs dotted about the place, leap up when they see someone and greet one warmly. I am soon sipping coffee. Up the road my 4 passengers, staff from the United Nations, are toiling away. I am not at liberty to join them but their group leader explains that they are visiting and assessing the progress of various UN projects in the Katakwe area.

This area, just to the north-east of Soroti, was badly affected by the recent flooding, and a constant stream of Russian-built helicopters flew in and out of this area for several weeks, dropping off vital relief supplies to those stranded there. Three of these helicopters are now parked at Soroti, their duty done until the next disaster strikes. The UN team will inspect the various projects it runs in the area's IDP camps and, later on, I will fly them to Pader, 40 minutes to the north-west. I think about the taxi driver who just told me that he would like to go back to school one day but that he has no money to do so, of the kids playing amidst the dirt and decay, and I pray that each project is successful. The UN team members are from Kenya, Holland and Finland (I think!) and have only a few hours, so MAF is a really valuable service to them, enabling them to complete a lot more work and cover a lot more 'area' than if they had to go by car.

(Deborah and Ivan welcoming mummy back home.)

Saturday 16 December 2007

I am sitting here beneath the wing of the 206 in a lazy sort of stupor, heavy eyelids, a body at rest and ready to have a little snooze. It is hot and humid and the birds cheep in a muted sort of way. I am parked at the top of a sloped runway, a road running past this threshold. Around 30 children have turned up to see the spectacle that the aircraft and I afford as we offload doctors and other personnel together with medical supplies and sample kits for CDC (centre for disease control). They sit there now, waiting for the next exciting instalment, happily chattering away as they poke sticks about and bounce younger siblings on their knees. Behind me the huge Ruwenzori Mountains rise upwards, the highest peak capped by snow. We flew over them a couple of hours earlier, descending down into the lush green valley below, the aircraft a small and insignificant winged speck against the granite mass. A huge river snaked its way alongside us, marking the border between the Congo and Western Uganda. It is all very lush and very green and smacks of the jungle. To the one side of the runway there is a swamp, its smelly green waters forever trying to invade the runway, a slippery muddy patch on the cut-grass airstrip evidence of the ongoing battle. The other side is a mess of 3m-high elephant grass and creeping vines. Looking down the runway I can just spy the odd camouflaged soldier with his AK-47. Overhead a deep drone as a Russian-built Antanov flies out towards the Congolese city, Goma. The dozy town of 'Bundi' isn't quite so dozy at the moment…

There are 2 immediate wars. One is very visible and loud and it is one which most of the people in the area have suffered through many times before. It is the renewed fighting between rebels and government forces as they try to take control of Goma. People die, have bits shot off, have their children rounded up and thrust into a uniform of one side or the other. This makes them friend or foe, depending upon which side of the gun they have been told to use their countrymen are standing. Small, frightened boys and girls soon become battle-hardened soldiers that fight for their own survival each day. Fathers and mothers, sons and daughters, homes and futures, all lost to a bullet.

The second is a war which is invisible. It has briefly terrified the local population as it is unseen and people do not always know how to fight back. It is the battle against the dreaded Ebola virus. There is no cure, its treatment being symptomatic. The pregnant and the old have no chance of survival, whilst several others do manage to fight their way to recovery. It crept into 'Bundi' several weeks ago. People suddenly started dying and no one knew why. Doctors and nurses were examining and attempting to treat the patients before they knew what they were dealing with. This has meant that some of the health workers have also contracted the virus. Two of the 4 doctors have contracted Ebola; one has died and the other has recovered. Some of the nurses are ill. The other 2 doctors, an American couple who have given the last 10 or so years of their lives to serving the needs of the ill in this area whilst trying to train up other doctors as well as run a small hospital, have 4 more days to go before they are given the all clear. I spent an hour at their home the other day so that we could share and encourage each other; the stress of waiting to find out whether they are ill or not, the heartbreak of losing their dear doctor friend to the disease, the enforced separation from their young children and the pressures of dealing with so many ill people was lined upon their faces. Life is suddenly on a thread. As the lady doctor told me: "We know God is with us, but losing our doctor friend has reminded us that it does not mean He will not let us die." The work of these doctors and nurses, and of the people we are flying in, has helped to halt the progress of the virus as well as reduce the overall panic among the local population.

Needless to say, it has been very busy in Operations as Adrian, Sarah and Carole try to juggle the usual flights with a flood of new requests from MSF (Medicine without Frontiers), CDC, the Ugandan Ministry of Health and the WHO (World Health Organisation.) The maintenance team has been working non-stop to try and keep our 4 aircraft flying and complete all the required maintenance as promptly as possible. The aircraft handling team has been super-busy refuelling and prepping the aircraft. God has been good to us in all of this and has even given us good weather. MAF has asked you all to pray. It has been a source of evangelism!!! The vast majority of the people we are flying are not Christian. When I pray before we fly I pray for their safety, I thank God for their work, I ask Him to protect them and their families. I then tell them that thousands of people around the world support MAF and that they are all praying for them! I get some very surprised looks and some wonderful responses! "Oh, thank you!" or "That is wonderful, thank you." I think that these people are actually very brave as they are, even fully-clothed in protective gear, still at risk of catching the disease, and yet they are there, helping these folk in many different ways. Christmas is here and, Christian or not, people still miss their families, and more so if they are so far from home. So, please do keep praying for them. Pray too that they will think on God this Christmas, see themselves as His and as part of His plan, and ask Him into their lives. Praise God, too, for the faithful service of the various members that go to make up our team out here in Uganda and for all those who pray and support this mission.

We are all looking forward to a hot and sunny Christmas. It is quite different here; not a Santa in sight and just a few scraps of tinsel here and there. Our prayer is that you all have a wonderful time this Christmas. Thank you all for your continued prayers and support. God bless, with much love, Mike, Deborah, Ivan and Laura.

PRAYER POINTS

❖ PRAISE GOD FOR A YEAR OF GOOD HEALTH FOR EACH MEMBER OF OUR FAMILY, FOR THOUSANDS OF SAFE FLYING HOURS AND HUNDREDS OF SAFE DRIVING HOURS.

❖ PRAISE GOD THAT DEBORAH AND IVAN HAVE CONTINUED TO SETTLE DOWN WELL INTO OUR FAMILY AND THAT THEY ARE BOTH HAPPY AT HOME AND AT SCHOOL.

❖ PRAISE GOD FOR KEEPING EACH ONE OF OUR LOVED ONES, IN VARIOUS PARTS OF THE WORLD, SAFE THIS YEAR.

❖ PRAISE AND THANK GOD FOR EACH SUPPORTER WHO MAKES IT POSSIBLE FOR US TO BE HERE AND FOR MAF TO DO THE WORK THAT IT DOES.

❖ PLEASE PRAY FOR OUR APPLICATION FOR LEGAL GUARDIANSHIP OVER DEBORAH AND IVAN: WE ARE AWAITING A COURT DATE, HOPEFULLY IN EARLY JANUARY. PRAY THAT WE BE AFFORDED LEGAL GUARDIANSHIP AS THIS GIVES DEBORAH AND IVAN GREATER LEGAL PROTECTION WITH RESPECT TO THEIR FUTURE WITH US AS A FAMILY.

❖ PRAY FOR US AS I SPEND A LOT OF TIME AWAY FROM HOME DURING 2008 AND FOR MIKE AND THE CHILDREN BACK HOME.

❖ PRAY FOR SUCCESS AND SAFETY IN ALL THE TRAINING I WILL NEED TO COMPLETE.

❖ PRAY FOR A CHURCH OR CELL GROUP THAT WILL COMMIT TO PRAY FOR OUR FAMILY, SPECIFICALLY IN

THE AREA OF SPIRITUAL PROTECTION, AT LEAST ONCE A WEEK WHEN WE MOVE TO MONGOLIA AS WE WILL BE IN A BUDDHIST/SHAMANIST COUNTRY WITH VERY FEW CHRISTIANS AROUND.

❖ PRAY FOR THE MISSIONARIES HERE IN UGANDA AND SUDAN, WHO FACE SUCH TRIALS OF PATIENCE AND PERSEVERANCE; SPECIFICALLY, UPHOLD WAYNE AND BEV OF CORNERSTONE FOUNDATION AND ASK THAT GOD WILL GRANT THEM FAVOUR WITH THE NGO BOARD SO THAT THEIR NGO CERTIFICATE WILL BE RENEWED WITHOUT FURTHER PROBLEMS.

❖ PLEASE PRAY FOR ADDITIONAL FINANCIAL SUPPORTERS: WE ARE ALL GOING TO NEED A LOT OF EXTRA-THICK WOOLLY COATS, ETC., FOR MONGOLIA.

LORD, WHERE WOULD YOU HAVE US BE? PLEASE SHOW US THE WAY FORWARD. THANK YOU FOR LEGAL GUARDIANSHIP OF D&I, THAT WAS A REAL BLESSING FROM YOU. I PRAISE YOU AND I THANK YOU FOR EACH DAY; IT IS HARD TO WAIT ON YOU; SORRY, BUT I MUST BE HONEST HERE. PLEASE HELP ME WAIT PATIENTLY AND HELP ME TO TRUST YOU, EVEN WHEN I HAVE NO IDEA OF WHAT IS NEXT. AMEN.

Dear Friends and Family: November 2007

One never knows quite what the day will hold and one never knows who you will get to fly. It was quite 'by chance' that, on Saturday, instead of flying a group to Kotido, I agreed to swap flights and flew a lady called Immaculee Ilibagiza to Pader instead. Tall and slender, and quite exhausted after a flight from the USA that took 3 days (she missed a connection in New York due to traffic, then had to change airlines, fly via Kenya, etc., etc., as Satan tried to stop her!), she stepped off from her Boeing and walked over to meet me at the little Cessna 206 that would take her to her final destination. As I often do, I asked her who she was and what she was doing in Uganda...

Immaculee is Rwandan and a survivor of the Rwandan genocide. During 1994 she and 7 other women spent 91 days squeezed into a tiny bathroom, scarcely breathing for fear of detection and slaughter. They hid in a minister's house; he was a Hutu and would have been required to kill each one of them had he been found hiding them. He, too, would have then been killed.

Immaculee explained to me that she learnt English using a dictionary whilst in that bathroom and that she "forged a profound and lasting relationship with God" during those months. Eventually, during the dead of night, they all managed to escape to a nearby French military 'safe' haven.

Immaculee has written a book on forgiveness, *Left to Tell*. At this very time in Uganda, former LRA rebels are touring the northern parts of Uganda, going from village to village, and asking for forgiveness. Immaculee, now working for the United Nations, was partnering with Frakes Productions, a Christian film company I believe to be documenting the proceedings. (See www.frakesproductions.com for clips of the LRA ceremony in Pader last weekend.) She made me think of Esther, who was brought to the palace "for such a time as this". I was really blessed by just speaking to her. We always pray before we fly and this was a very special time for both of us. Please uphold her and the Christian film team. God makes amazing people!

Below are 2 links, the first a 60-minute interview with Immaculee, the second the website for her first book.

http://www.cbsnews.com/stories/2006/11/30/60minutes/main2218371.shtml

http://www.lefttotell.com/

Below is an email article on the peace talks:

http://www.irinnews.org/report.aspx?reportid=60001 (this is a UN site.)

With respect to the peace talks, it is difficult to know what to write about. On one hand an LRA delegation is going around asking for forgiveness using *mato put*, a traditional Acholi ritual that involves the slaughtering of goats, stepping over them, etc. The church, I am told, is very much involved in the process. On the other hand, the newspaper states that the chief propagandist for President Mugabe (Zimbabwe) is a main player of this delegation. It is hard to know what to think and the reports from the ground vary widely. Please do pray for this whole thing; that it will be a Godly peace and forgiveness, not a pact with the devil or peace at any cost. There are reports of folk going back to their villages and having nightmares, not sleeping, etc. - the trauma involved is very real and very intense. There are a lot of deeply traumatized people out there and many of them simply do not know God; do pray for the missionaries 'out there'. Here is a link that talks about *mato put*:

http://www.religionnewsblog.com/16031/lords-resistance-army

On a quite different front but in the same area, Mike and Wayne Stevens (Cornerstone Foundation, Australia) are up in Kitgum for 2 weeks whilst all of this is going on. Personally, I am quite thrilled that they have gone up in the midst of peace talks and forgiveness ceremonies; one was held in Kitgum the day they arrived (Friday last week). But it is quite an uphill battle. A pastor who has worked for an NGO there for 17 years has just been found out, having basically stolen land, buildings, etc. from the NGO. He has been well cared for, along with his family, and been trained, sent abroad 10 times and fully trusted. Please pray for the lady who heads up this

NGO as she deals with the heartbreak of betrayal and the implications of losing land, buildings, etc.

As for 'the boys' (as we like to refer to Mike And Wayne!), they are wading through lies and half-truths, finding that many items have been stolen from the property, that those left in charge have stolen the money, have used other money for their own ends, have been dishonest and disloyal. Please do pray for them, that they would have a God-given spirit of discernment as well as grace in abundance. Wisdom, patience and perseverance would also come in handy! They are living on the local diet of beans and posho (maize porridge) and Mike's ample supply of biscuits!!! Bev and I are holding the fort this side of Uganda, trying to keep them encouraged and their spirits up and give 'unbiased' advice/input where required and ask them not to throttle anyone. Deborah is ill with a bad bout of 'flu and a chest infection, so please pray for her healing. HM Queen Elizabeth II arrives next week and so many of the roads are already closed, including those to the doctor. We are both a bit bleary-eyed from lack of sleep due to nights spent coughing and crying, so a speedy recovery is prayed for. And just to add a final, special touch, Mike and I head off to Mongolia on 26 November. Mike is due back on the 24th, cutting it a bit fine!

There is a need for a pilot in Mongolia. There has been for some time now and we feel that we would like to consider moving there at the end of 2008. MAF works here as Blue Sky Aviation for various reasons. It will be a HUGE change for us. They have lovely summers at +40°C and even better winters at

-40°C. We would get to live in a Communist-built flat in Ulaanbaatar. We are going on a 'look-see' visit. PLEASE pray that God will speak very clearly to us. We will need to leave Deborah and Ivan behind with Wayne and Bev for the duration. We leave on the 26th, arrive 3 days later on the 28th. We return to Uganda, leaving on 6 December, arriving on the 7th. Please do pray for our little ones at this time; for Wayne and Bev as they look after them, for us as we travel and then 'experience' Mongolia. The link for the company is below:

http://www.blueskyaviation.mn The interesting bit is that the warmest things either of us owns are jeans, trainers and a thin jumper! Anyone have a spare Yak jacket or Arctic boots?! This is also quite tough for our extended families, so please do pray for them as well. One cannot exactly nip over and visit the kids in Mongolia!

Finally, many thanks for the many emails we have received of late; it is always encouraging to hear from folk and to read about what you are all up to.

We pray that you are all well and send our best wishes and love.

God bless, with much love, Mike, D&I and Laura.

Lord, people here are desperate for peace. This land cries out for peace, the people are desperate for peace, even the Earth cries out for rest from the blood that is spilt upon her. Thousands upon thousands of people's lives rest on the decisions of one or two madmen, bent on evil. Lord, move into the hearts of these men and change them. That or remove their influence.

I pray against witchcraft and all the rituals involved. Strengthen Your Church so that she may stand firm at this time. Embolden her so that she will be able boldly and confidently to proclaim the way forward. Pour out Your wisdom upon her leaders so that they may correctly and carefully lead Your people forward and that they may, by Your grace and in Your strength, bring many into a knowledge of You and Your ways.

I pray for all missionaries out here who seek to be Your hands and eyes and heart. And I pray for all those back home who support all missionaries - keep them strong as they help keep us strong. Bless them, encourage them and strengthen them. Amen.

First week of January 2008.

A lthough quite a small country, Uganda has rather varied vegetation. To the west and south-west, the glacier-topped Ruwenzori mountain range that embraces the jungles which support gorillas and other primates, together with a host of other endangered species of wildlife. To the north-east, however, it is very different. Here, the barren and dusty plains that make up the Karamoja. It is a vast area of sweeping plains that are tinged green after rains but boast that tawny lion colour the rest of the year. Every now and then a range of mountains rise from the earth, stretching upwards towards the sky, rugged and foreboding, long, sleeping dragons with an air of :"Do not disturb" about them.

It is that time of year again. Now the dragons puff smoke from smouldering nostrils as people set the plains alight. Huge fires rapidly gnaw their way through the dry grass, fanning out to turn the veld into a patchwork of black on brown. Smoke fills the air, so much so that it is becomes like flying through pea soup. Dry winds and mountains generate turbulence, throwing the aircraft about, her hapless passengers all trying desperately not to 'make milkshake'. Temperatures soar, rising to around 35-40°C, and dust invades everything. It is the 'dry season'.

Linda and Philip Byler of African Inland Mission (AIM) live in Torrit, Sudan, just north-west of the Karamoja. Philip is the general manager of AIM, Sudan. I flew in to take him and his wife to a conference in Kampala and got invited to tea! It was great. There we sat, sipping the sweet, spicy African chai under the shade of a very basic concrete-and-thatch homestead surrounded by suitcases and the detritus of Christmas 2007. One has to admire those who live in such hot places and in such basic conditions. Matt, a young American teacher, arrives and announces that he is back early from school as none of his students has turned up. No one is quite sure when they will return. Here, time is different. The team help out in many ways in this part of Sudan. Education, language training, water projects, you name it!

Dad and Daughter of ABC.

I flew this father-and-daughter team into Lira. This American-run NGO raises money in the USA to provide microfinance opportunities for people in Lira. X has come to make a film that will show who is receiving the help, why and the difference it is making. He intends to use the film to raise awareness and so raise more funding; Y is on her first trip to Africa. The two visited numerous people in Lira who are benefitting from the microfinance scheme to see how they were faring. All people shared and showed only positive, life-enriching success stories! People who had started small chicken farms, had bought a bike/taxi, etc. and were now self-sufficient and supporting their families. That night, the two interviewed various prostitutes in the street. X shared with me the next day how he and his daughter, together with these ladies, had sat together on the kerb, all in tears, as they listened to the various life stories of these ladies. Many of these ladies will offer their services simply for a single plate of beans or porridge. The team hopes to be able to raise more funding, to be able to give some of these ladies an opportunity to start a new life.

The following day I flew Dr Sahar from Kaabong, Karamoja, to Kampala. Dr Sahar is a young Swedish lady of Iranian descent, working as a paediatric doctor in the Kaabong hospital. She is the only doctor and works as a part of the *Médicins sans Frontières* (MSF) team. She shared with me some of the joy and some of the heartbreak of working in her hospital. It has no running water, some very poorly-motivated and unenthusiastic staff who may or may not turn up for work, hordes of malnourished children and a generally very low standard of living. The doctor showed me photos of some of the children under her care, smiling broadly as she looked at those children who had recovered and were now fit and well. I was so touched by her compassion and her obvious and deep care for the many children who came through her doors. I was flying the doctor to Kampala, from where she would fly to Tanzania to help do some training at a hospital there during her holidays!

10 January.

The turmoil in Kenya has left Uganda with fuel shortages. Uganda is landlocked and so heavily reliant on the road and rail network in and out of Kenya. Petrol soared to around £2.50/litre and diesel to around

£1.75/litre, when you could find any, severely restricting where and what the average person could do and making travel simply impossible for the poor. Entebbe International Airport was unable to give us any fuel for around a week. Thankfully, we had reserves at Kajjansi, but other operators were forced to cancel some of their flights. Thankfully, a few tankers have managed to get through now, so we hope and pray that things will slowly start to return to normal. Please do pray for the many people stranded out in the countryside post-Christmas; many had to delay returning to Kampala as they could not afford the huge increase in bus-fare, others simply had to pay it and put themselves in debt.

And so, 2008 has got off to an interesting start! We do hope and pray that you are all keeping well and not too cold and wet up there in the floods. Thank you for your continued prayers for this region and for the many varied groups of NGOs, missions, etc. working out here.

Mike, Deborah, Ivan and I all went to the High Court on the 14th. We are applying for legal guardianship of the children, as this affords them much greater protection in the future. The judge, who has been very ill and whom we were warned may not be able to attend for health reasons, did in fact attend. It was an hour-long process during which our lawyer was grilled and the children had to sit still and be quiet. Both Mike and I had been ill the entire weekend with food poisoning (by God's good grace neither of the children got it!) and it also activated latent giardia that I did not know I had, so we were both pretty tired. Mike and I really believe that the Lord did something special for us on the 14th. The judge arrived, she was also not late, the children were fantastically well-behaved, we survived a nightmare traffic-jam and got to the court on time, and both Mike and I were indeed well enough to not need to dash off to the nearest loo at any point. It is so encouraging to see God move gently yet powerfully in our lives. We await the ruling which will be given this Monday. Many thanks to you all for praying for us and please share our encouragement at how He has answered them.

Happy New Year!

With much love and thanks, Mike, D&I and Laura.

Lord, please bring peace to Kenya. So many killed, so many disfigured and mutilated. Please hold back the tidal wave of anger and hatred that is sweeping through Kenya. Help people to work through the issues and grievances they have with one another, tribe against tribe. Raise up many gifted in reconciliation and give them space and opportunity to minister healing and forgiveness in Your name.

Please be with MAF Kenya's team; please help those of different tribes within the MAF Kenya team to be 'different'; to stay loving and caring towards each other. Hold the harmony. I pray especially for Jane Wambui (MAF pilot) as she has to fly all over Kenya and mix with many tribes, not all friendly towards her.

Please protect Uganda from this unrest; guard her people from the same things and please prevent the hatred and discord from spreading over here. Amen.

News from Mike and Laura: April 2008

In Africa there is something unique about the smell and even the feel of the air, once it has rained. I found myself marvelling at this unique freshness as I walked back to my room from the MAF  hangar in Lanseria, South Africa. Grey, smudgy skies above, their clouds empty of rain, scurried across the horizon, spent ballerinas leaving centre stage. Around me big puddles of fresh water quickly transformed into bathing areas as crowds of small birds splashed about in them, cleaning their delicate feathers and quenching their thirst. On the tip of each blade of grass a tiny diamond, shining as it slid slowly down its host. With each step mud splattered onto my flying trousers, but I didn't mind: I was back in Africa and I felt a huge smile creep across my face. I looked past the busy runway, taking in the glorious African panorama and thought: "How great Thou art!"

It has been a busy year! Yesterday I returned from North America. I have been away for 2 months. Mike and the children have spent that time in South Africa, staying with his mum whilst we were apart. The children have been in school there, 'Granny' has been getting to know her grandchildren very well and Mike has been using each opportunity not only to tell folk about MAF but also to encourage young adults in the churches as to their own mission. We all met up at Johannesburg airport, a flurry of hugs and tears, before flying back to Uganda together. I left Idaho at 7am on Sunday morning with the aircraft's wings covered in snow. We arrived back in Uganda on Tuesday night at 9pm and stepped out into a warm and balmy night. What a contrast! And once again I marvelled at the blessing that aviation is; 3 days in the air may sound a lot, but it would have been months of travel by boat and then some sort of donkey trek across mountains and rivers and lion-infested plains for the original missionaries! And all that in a long skirt!!!

As we shared in our last newsletter, Mike and I have felt the Lord calling us to Mongolia to fly there with MAF under the name of Blue Sky Aviation. I have been in South Africa completing one of MAF's specialised courses and then in the USA obtaining the necessary licences to allow me to fly the American-registered aircraft that we use in Mongolia. It has been a very demanding time: for Mike as he cared for the children and all that goes with that, and for me as I studied and flew extensively. We missed each other terribly! But we praise and thank God for His wonderful goodness as we are all safely back together and I passed all the courses. I will be heading off to Mongolia in mid-May, returning to Uganda in mid-July, so as to initially complete further MAF specialised training and then take over from the lone pilot there, who will be going on furlough. Once again Mike will be alone with the children, staying on in Uganda, so please do continue praying for us. We have many other challenging requirements to meet before we are able to move out to Mongolia as a family at the end of 2008. A lot of it involves working with the authorities in both Uganda and the UK as we work towards full legal adoption of Deborah and Ivan, and so we do ask for you to cover us in prayer. What we have achieved this year as a family is something along the lines of parting the Red Sea, and so we know we are in His will but we are also so very aware that we need your prayers and support at this time.

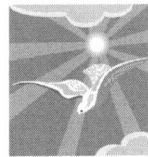 There have been numerous moments when we have seen the hand of God at work, and it is very exciting!

❖ Whilst in America I had to find a church to attend. I noticed a board outside a building advertising Vineyard Fellowship Church, so I went there. I had a wonderful time of fellowship with this small group of people. The pastor, Kurt, is passionate about mission and he and a team of 5 others have all just left for a remote part of Mexico. They will be working with a long-term mission couple who live there and serve that community. The short-term team will be doing whatever they are asked to, whether it be building work, evangelism, teaching, etc. We all prayed for them as they left; I was just so excited to pray for folk going out, knowing not only what a blessing they would be to the community but also the encouragement that they would be to the mission couple living out there.

❖ On my flight back, somewhere over the Atlantic, the purser asked if there was a doctor on board. Around 30 minutes later she announced that a lady had just given birth to a little girl! I felt the Lord prompt me to go and give my necklace, a gold cross given to me by Mike for my birthday 3 years ago, to the baby. I thought it silly. A short while later I went to the bathroom and there, to my surprise, was a lady holding the new baby. I put my hand on the baby and silently prayed for her, for her life and that God would be in it. Suddenly the baby's parents were there. They were a Muslim couple, the mother being covered from head-to-toe, so I took off the necklace and gave it to her, saying it was for her baby. The mother was thrilled. Please do pray that God will work in their lives, that as she looks at the cross she will become aware that when Mohammed says in the Koran that one must find The Way, by finding Christ she will find The Way and a whole lot more besides.

❖ Whilst I was in America my brother was in a horrific car crash. Both cars were totally demolished. Ward, my brother, had head injuries and has had to have 3 operations so far. The impact of the crash moved his eye; they have had to take his eye out during one of the operations, put cartilage from his ear under the eye, and then replace the eye. He is doing well and well on the road to a full recovery. But I am so aware that God has kept him and I thank Him for that.

Please do pray for him as well as his wife and 3-year-old son at this really tough time.

As for the MAF flying side of things….

October 2007

One never knows quite what the day will hold and one never knows who one will get to fly. It was quite by chance that, on Saturday, instead of flying a group to Kotido, I agreed to swap flights and flew a lady called Immaculee Ilibagiza to Pader instead. Tall and slender and quite exhausted after a flight from the USA that took 3 days (she missed a connection in New York due to traffic, then had to change airlines, fly via Kenya, etc., etc., as Satan tried to stop her!), she stepped from her Boeing and walked over to meet me at the little Cessna 206 that would take her to her final destination. As I often do, I asked her who she was and what she was doing in Uganda…

Immaculee is Rwandan and a survivor of the Rwandan genocide. During 1994 she and 7 other women spent 91 days squeezed into a tiny bathroom, scarcely breathing for fear of detection and slaughter. They hid in a minister's house; he was a Hutu and would have been required to kill each one of them had he been found hiding them. He, too, would have then been killed.

Immaculee explained to me that she learnt English using a dictionary whilst in that bathroom, and that she "forged a profound and lasting relationship with God" during those months. Eventually, during the dead of night, they all managed to escape to a nearby French military 'safe' haven.

Immaculee has written a book on forgiveness, *Left to Tell*. At this very time in Uganda, former LRA rebels are touring the northern parts of Uganda, going from village to village, and asking for forgiveness. Immaculee, now working for the United Nations, was partnering with Frakes Productions, a Christian film company I believe to be documenting the proceedings. (See www.frakesproductions.com for clips of the LRA ceremony in Pader last weekend.) She made me think of Esther, who was brought to the palace "for such a time as this". I was really blessed by just speaking to her. We always pray before we fly and this was a very special time for the both of us. Please uphold her and the Christian film team. God makes amazing people!

November 2007

Although quite a small country, Uganda has rather varied vegetation. To the west and south-west, the glacier-topped Ruwenzori mountain range that embraces the jungles which support gorillas and other primates, together with a host of other endangered species of wildlife. To the north-east, however, it is very different. Here, the barren and dusty plains that make up the Karamoja. It is a vast area of sweeping plains that are tinged green after rains but boast that tawny lion colour the rest of the year. Every now and then a range of mountains rise from the earth, stretching upwards towards the sky, rugged and foreboding, long, sleeping dragons with an air of: "Do not disturb" about them.

It is that time of year again. Now the dragons puff smoke from smouldering nostrils as people set the plains alight. Huge fires rapidly gnaw their way through the dry grass, fanning out to turn the 'veld' into a patchwork of black on brown. Smoke fills the air so much so that it is becomes like flying through pea soup. Dry winds and mountains generate turbulence, throwing the aircraft about, her hapless passengers all trying desperately not to 'make milkshake'. Temperatures soar, rising to around 35-40°C and dust invades everything. It is the 'dry season'.

Linda and Philip Byler of African Inland Mission (AIM) live in Torrit, Sudan, just north-west of the Karamoja. Philip is the general manager of AIM, Sudan. I flew in to take him and his wife to a conference in Kampala and got invited to tea! It was great. There we sat, sipping the sweet, spicy African chai under the shade of a very basic concrete-and-thatch homestead surrounded by suitcases and the detritus of Christmas 2007. One has to admire those who live in such hot places and in such basic conditions. Matt, a young American teacher, arrives and announces that he is back early from school as none of his students has turned up. No one is quite sure when they will return. Here, time is different. The team help out in many ways in this part of Sudan. Education, language training, water projects, you name it!

December 2007

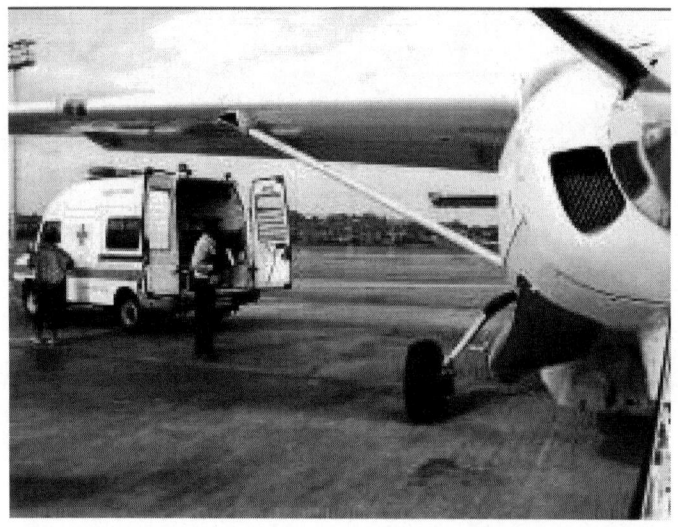

There was an Ebola outbreak in the far west of Uganda. The very word 'Ebola' makes anyone in the medical profession shudder. It is an extremely contagious disease, one without cure that ruthlessly and mercilessly ravages any community it is introduced to. It was all concentrated in the Bundibugyio area where our good mission partner, World Harvest Mission (WHM), is based. There are 4 doctors in the area, 2 of them being a couple (with children) from America. Both parents were exposed to the virus but neither contracted it. The 2 other doctors, both Ugandan, contracted the disease. One of them, a dear friend of the WHM couple, died, leaving a pregnant wife and 3 children. The other doctor survived. A large percentage of the nursing staff contracted the disease and perished. MAF stepped into the breach and we flew WHO and MSF medical teams in and out almost daily. Through the work of these brave medical teams, enabled by MAF, the disease was contained within around 4 weeks. Instead of the usual hundreds of people dying, only 35 perished. It was over Christmas and so MAF also used this as an opportunity to reach out to these medical teams, most of whom are not Christians, by letting them know that many people around the world were praying for them as well as sending down some special Christmas goodies. Please pray that each of them will come to know Christ.

January 2008

2 weeks ago I flew Trevor, a BBC reporter, up to Kotido in the Karamoja area. Kotido is in the far north-east of Uganda; its people are related to the Masaai and Turkana in Kenya and Sudan. The Karamajong peoples still live a very traditional lifestyle, having retained many aspects of their original culture but having adopted numerous aspects of the 'western' culture. Trevor and I spent the day with Oxfam. The Oxfam office is run by various different people groups from Uganda, with the majority being from the Karamoja area. They run health, hygiene

and finance training, try to encourage parents to send their children to school, give HIV/AIDS counselling, etc. We drove around 30 minutes out into the 'bush' with the Director and another staff member to visit one of the *manyattas*. A *manyatta* is a collection of traditional huts, a large open area for the housing of cattle at night in the centre, all surrounded by a very thick stick fence around 7ft high.

On arrival we found a group of young men sleeping under the trees. Children magically appeared, mostly under 5. In the far distance you could make out a line of women walking towards us, each carrying a bundle of sticks weighing around 50kg on their heads. It was scorching hot.

We crawled through the low openings of the stick wall and entered the *manyatta*. It was quite deserted. Where were the people, we wondered? Well, we asked.

The young men were sleeping outside, the older men we located in one of the main huts, all gathered around in the dark, drinking. It was 10am and most were well on their way to being drunk. Two little boys of around 5 were 'minding' the men; i.e. helping them to stagger out the low door of the hut and leading them to the nearest fence, where they would relieve themselves. The place stank of stale 'beer', sweat and urine. The leader of this group appeared from somewhere, the proud owner of a scarred face, a scarred body and eyes as hard and cold as steel. The main focus of these groups is cattle; they raid, often killing, rival people for their cattle and so many are adorned with scars from the various battles they have been in. Only a few weeks prior, an Oxfam employee had been tragically killed in a raid - he had been in the wrong place at the wrong time. We were told that the men sleep, raid and drink.

The ladies live a very different life. They have no choice in whom they marry; they are sold-off by fathers for around 100 cattle to a husband. More often than not they will be one of his many wives located over the surrounding area. They do just about everything. Before she can marry, she must prove that she can build the fence and the house. She must be fit and strong. Girls who are uneducated fetch a higher 'bride price' for their fathers and so education of girls is rare. She also does all the cooking, makes the beer, serves the men and so forth. When I asked them what they wanted most, they said "peace"; that the raiding would stop.

As for the children, well, the girls shadow their mothers until around 15, when they marry. The boys stay with their mothers until around 6, at which point they go off to herd goats. At around 12 they are sent off to herd and care for the precious family cattle, often spending months away from home, sleeping out beneath the stars.

Please do pray for the work of Oxfam. I know that I would not want to live that lifestyle and felt very blessed to have been given an education, taught about God,

203

given the opportunity to reach for my dreams and have the chance to marry the man I wanted to.

As a westerner I guess I help in the 'meddling' with another's culture. I thought about how, just under 200 years ago, children and women had very few rights in the UK, the poor being especially vulnerable to exploitation. That culture changed. Do I pray for this one to change?

A few days later I flew Sean Farrel from Trocaire (Irish for 'compassion'), Uganda. He was going to Kotido on behalf of the Catholic Church in Ireland, looking at setting up a project there that would help in this area. One of the projects was to help women be in a position to inherit. The current policy when the husband dies is that she does not inherit, but is inherited; he was asked: "How can property own property?" Please do pray for him as he looks into this area; that he will be given great wisdom and sensitivity.

In January we, as a family, also finally went to the High Court, where our application for Legal Guardianship over Deborah and Ivan was heard. This gives the children much greater protection should anything ever happen to Mike and me and so was very important to us. The Judge granted us legal guardianship! Thank you to everyone who prayed for us and encouraged us.

And finally…

We are in the UK on furlough during April and May of this year. We arrive in the UK on 18 April.

We will be at Cheriton Baptist Church, Kent, on Sunday 20 April at 1030hrs.

On Saturday 26th we will be talking at a MAF event in Plymouth.

On Sunday 27th we will be at Living Waters Church in Paignton, Torbay.

On Friday 1 May we will be talking at a cell group meeting in Tunbridge Wells.

Sunday 3 May we will be talking in Braintree, Essex.

We will visit South Ashford Baptist Church on 4 May before Mike and children fly out to Uganda and I leave for Mongolia via China.

We hope and pray that we will get to meet many of you. Please do feel free to email me for further info on any of these locations and I will obtain the information as soon as possible and send it to you.

Thank you so much for what you help make possible in the smallest, most forgotten places of the world.

Psalm 115:1.

God bless you. With our sincere love and deep appreciation,

Mike, Deborah, Ivan and Laura.

Mike 'puppeteering'

Deborah and Ivan playing

Lord, thank You for Mike! Thank You for his support, his strength, his love. It would all be so sadly different without him; thank You for keeping him safe on the roads as he drives all over the place for so many people. It's so good to see him puppeteering! Thank You for D&I; they are funny and cuddly and cute and difficult all at once. Thank You that they are settled into the family now, that they are doing well at school, that they have friends, and that they are so healthy. Lord, You are good to us

and have blessed us and I thank You and praise You for that.
Amen.

Kuron peace Village
www.peaceviallage.com
13 April 2008

There are times when I am totally awestruck by the enormity of the vision God gives certain people. My 2-day trip to Kuron, Sudan, near the border with Ethiopia, brought me into contact with one of these mighty warriors of God.

I flew 3 people, 2 Belgian men (Louwrens and Michael) and a Sudanese lady (Prisca), from Entebbe to Kuron, a 3-hour flight that would have taken 3 days using a 4x4. Our little metal bird swooped out of a charcoal-grey sky, alighting on a narrow, dirt strip at the base of green-cloaked granite hills. We were met by a small herd of unimpressed goats, a few bemused goatherds and a selection of budding thorn trees. Dust clouds announced the arrival of Bishop Taban in his truck, followed closely by a soldier armed with a tripod-mounted gun and a Kalashnikov to guard the aircraft.

Bishop Taban, a 5'3" powerhouse of 72, was all smiles and handshakes, the snow-white hair and beard giving the impression of forgotten shaving foam precariously balancing upon his head. We all piled into his vehicle and slowly negotiated what remains of the dirt road between the airstrip and his compound. We crossed over a bridge which he had erected so as to enable people to come and go, but which is now also used by tanks and other armoured vehicles crossing from Ethiopia into Sudan.

The rains of recent weeks had graced everything with a tint of lush green and temporarily relieved some of the worst of the dust. Pastoralists dozed about in the sun, their AK-47s and bows & arrows propped up against a rock pile, as their cattle nibbled contentedly upon bushes and grass shoots. It hummed of war and peace.

Michael and his team, part of 'Friends of Sister Immanuel of Cairo', were on a visit to assess what needs this charity could help meet. Their main focus is on child education and the charity supports schools all over the world, including one in Masindi, Uganda. Well, they had a lot to see!

Bishop Taban's vision was to build what he calls a peace village. The area, in common with many parts of Africa, is wracked by war. If not war as we know it, then inter-tribal war. The Taposa peoples, similar to the Masaai and Karamajong peoples, form a large percentage of the local population. As with the Karamajong, the Taposa prize their cattle as an indicator of wealth and status. A lot of time and effort goes into caring for their cattle and stealing ('raiding') cattle from neighbouring groups. In order to marry, a young man will need to 'raid' 60-100 cows in order to purchase his bride. The price is so high as the women do absolutely everything. This includes building the homes, all the domestics, bearing children, fetching water, etc. Men obviously try to protect their cattle from theft and so most cattle 'raids' result in loss of life and/or serious injury somewhere along the line. This is all in addition to the regular war. Bishop Taban has built a small compound which has a school, a lean-to dispensary, a 'clinic' and several little *tukuls* (huts) that form accommodation for the staff. He has encouraged small villages to settle in the area, the demonstration farm he manages being a great incentive. He encourages people from different faiths, cultures, genders, etc. to live in harmony.

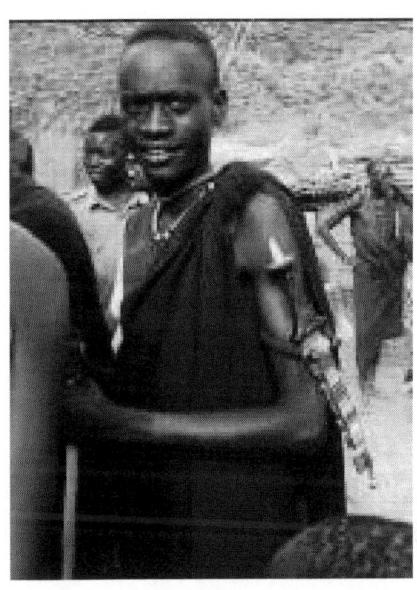

Intrigued, I asked the Bishop how he had come about the idea. A prisoner of war during the 1962-1975 war, he had seen many acts of cruelty but had used the opportunity to minister to Muslims and Christians alike. He was also fortunate enough to grow up in a village near Torit, Sudan, where the British had a sawmill. The British hired people from numerous different tribes and so he grew up with friends from a wide range of backgrounds. The Bishop related to me how he only came to know of 'tribes' once he had left that area. He also visited a co-operative in Israel where Palestinians (both Christian and Muslim) and Jews all live together in peace. What started there with a handful of families has grown into a large co-operative of around 1000 families! He said that when he saw it he felt that he wanted to try and do that in his country and so set about doing just that.

Life in the villages is lived in a way we simply do not. Seasons, daylight and rains all dictate the pace and direction of the daily routine. Men travel miles with their cattle, oblivious of man-made borders, often away for months at a time in search of grazing. Ladies and youngsters go out in long caravans, babies in baskets slung over the backs of stubborn donkeys, to take them supplies as needed. Old ladies and young children remain behind to care for the goats and the villages.

We visited one of the villages in the valley, instantly surrounded by men and children, some friendly, some less so. A debate broke out as to my gender: how could it be possible that a woman could fly? Was she really a woman? It took some time for the Bishop to explain that I was. Children cautiously approach us to touch our pale skin, squealing with delight as we show them their photos on our digital cameras. Ladies appear, bodies decorated with special scars, bits of plastic, ring-pulls off coke cans (yep, even here you find Coke!) and traditional beads. They hold your hand and excitedly share their news and I nod politely and smile, none the wiser.

Later we climb a small mountain to visit a village on top. It is deserted, bar 2 old ladies and a small girl. Goats with tiny, newborn kids, their bells clanking as they move, turn to acknowledge us. A rat scurries past. A pot on a fire, with something I can't identify in it, boils and bubbles away. The ladies are thrilled to see the Bishop and start to dance and sing and the girl starts to wail. The view is breathtaking and you feel as if you have stepped back several hundred years and stumbled upon something an explorer of old would have found.

Near the compound a proper clinic is in the process of being built. Michael asks if it will be completed this year as it has been several years in the making. The Bishop explains that, as the building equipment and supplies have not already made it through it is unlikely, as very soon the dirt road will become unusable, especially for big trucks. It is hard to explain to a person from a very task-orientated culture why this task is not yet done! Inside the shell of the building a pile of wood waits to be transformed into some part of the roof. For the moment it has become a store for a large leg of raw cow...

A village that encourages peace, teaches reconciliation, provides schooling and medical care, teaches agriculture and promotes Christianity. All in some isolated and obscure part of Sudan!

It was a real experience and a real adventure. It was a demonstration of how a person can give an entire lifetime to something that they believe in and plod on regardless. It was also a reminder of how big a difference support from 'outside' really is, and just what a difference it can and does make.

Dear Friends and Family: 8 March 2008

Well, this is a tough subject! I have had a lot of exposure to the hot topic of 'culture' of late. Do pray for wisdom as we deal with it all!

2 weeks ago I flew Trevor, a BBC reporter, up to Kotido in the Karamoja area. Kotido is in the far north-east of Uganda; its people are related to the Masaai and Turkana in Kenya and Sudan. The Karamajong peoples still live a very traditional lifestyle, having retained many aspects of their original culture but having adopted numerous aspects of the 'western' culture.

Trevor and I spent the day with Oxfam. The Oxfam office is run by various different people groups from Uganda, with the majority being from the Karamoja area. They run health, hygiene and finance training, try to encourage parents to send their children to school, give HIV/AIDS counselling, etc. We drove around 30 minutes out into the 'bush' with the Director and another staff member to visit one of the *manyattas*. A *manyatta* is a collection of traditional huts, a large open area for the housing of cattle at night in the centre, all surrounded by a very thick stick fence around 7ft high.

On arrival we found a group of young men sleeping under the trees. Children magically appeared, mostly under 5. In the far distance you could make out a line of women walking towards us, each carrying a bundle of sticks weighing around 50kg on their heads. It was scorching hot.

We crawled through the low openings of the stick wall and entered the *manyatta*. It was quite deserted. Where were the people, we wondered? Well, we asked.

The young men were sleeping outside; the older men we located in one of the main huts, all gathered around in the dark, drinking. It was 10am and most were well on their way to being drunk. Two little boys of around 5 were 'minding' the men, i.e. helping them to stagger out the low door of the hut and leading them to the nearest fence, where they would relieve themselves. The place stank of stale 'beer', sweat and urine. The leader of this group appeared from somewhere, the proud owner of a scarred face, a scarred body and eyes as hard and cold as steel. The main focus of these groups is cattle; they raid, often killing rival people for their cattle, and so many are adorned with scars from the various battles they have been in. Only a few weeks prior an Oxfam employee had been tragically killed in a raid - he had been in the wrong place at the wrong time. We were told that the men sleep, raid and drink.

The ladies live a very different life. They have no choice in whom they marry; they are sold-off by fathers for around 100 cattle to a husband. More often than not they will be one of his many wives located over the surrounding area. They do just about everything. Before she can marry, she must prove that she can build the fence and the house. She must be fit and strong. Girls who are uneducated fetch a higher 'bride price' for their fathers and so education of girls is rare. She also does all the cooking, makes the beer, serves the men and so forth. When I asked them what they wanted most, they said "peace"; that the raiding would stop.

As for the children, well, the girls shadow their mothers until around 15, when they marry. The boys stay with their mothers until around 6, at which point they go off to herd goats. At around 12 they are sent off to herd and care for the precious family cattle, often spending months away from home, sleeping out beneath the stars.

Please do pray for the work of Oxfam. I know that I would not want to live that lifestyle and felt very blessed to have been given an education, taught about God, given the opportunity to reach for my dreams and have the chance to marry the man I wanted to.

As a westerner I guess I help in the 'meddling' with another's culture. I thought about how, just under 200 years ago, children and women had very few rights in the UK, the poor being especially vulnerable to exploitation. That culture changed. Do I pray for this one to change?

A few days later I flew Sean Farrel from Trocaire (Irish for 'compassion'), Uganda. He was going to Kotido on behalf of the Catholic Church in Ireland, looking at setting-up a project there that would help in this area. One of the projects was to help women be in a position to inherit. The current policy when the husband dies is that she does not inherit but is inherited; he was asked: "How can property own property?" Please do pray for him as he looks into this area; that he will be given great wisdom and sensitivity.

The problems in Kenya are terrible. The papers are filled with gruesome photos of charred and hacked bodies. Bombs were found on railway tracks here in Uganda, just down the road in Jinja next to a fuel depot. The violence appears to slowly spreading this way. Many of our team were in Kenya on holiday in December and were forced to leave their cars there and fly back; their cars are still there! The borders are often closed and very dangerous places at the moment. Please do pray for the MAF team in Nairobi, as well as for the many other people caught up in this nightmare. Please pray for peace to return to this region. Yesterday I flew a group of people from MSF to Amudat, a town on the Ugandan/Kenyan border. They had had to fly as driving was considered too dangerous.

I had 3 Uganda passengers for Sudan yesterday. I flew Edward and Rachel of AVSI to Ikotos, Sudan, yesterday. Rachel and Edward had been on a week's leave in Kampala. Rachel teaches people about landmines; how to avoid being injured by them, what they look like, where they are, etc. Many people, especially children, are still killed or maimed each year by unwittingly walking onto a landmine. I also flew Annette of LWF to Sudan; she went into Torit where she will be helping the team to set up independently of the LWF team in Uganda.

Two days ago there was a special flight. I flew 8 people from the World Harvest Mission team back into Bundibugio. We had flown many out because of the Ebola outbreak. It was so good to be able to fly them back in, many of whom were children rejoining their families. Thank you, God, for bringing healing and recovery to that area!

Last week we received a ruling from the High Court of Uganda; Mike and I have been granted Legal Guardianship of Deborah and Ivan! Many thanks to all of you who prayed for this; we are thrilled. It gives our children greater legal protection and is another step towards adoption.

Mike and the children leave for South Africa on the 4th February. They will be gone for 6 weeks. They will fly down via Dodoma in Tanzania. Please do pray for a safe trip and a good time in SA. I leave for a different part of SA on 19 February. I will be there for 2 weeks, completing an MAF course that I need to do for Mongolia. Please do pray that I will be successful in the course, and for safe flights and protection whilst there. After that I leave for the USA for 3 weeks where I am doing American flying licence exams. The aircraft I will be flying in Mongolia later this year is American-registered, so I need American licences to fly it! It is a huge workload - I rather feel like I am climbing Everest in my slippers, so please do pray. And please do pray for our children as the family is apart for just less than 2 months. And pray for Mike!!! If it all goes a bit quiet on the email side of things, do forgive us...

Until then, God bless you and our thanks for all those prayers you offer; He is answering them!

Best wishes and much love, Mike and Laura and D&I.

Lord, it is difficult to always see through others' glasses when mine fit so much better! I find it hard to see much good in some cultures and very hard to see it from their perspective. I don't like to know girls are sold off for a few cows to a man who has several wives already. I don't like to know that girls are not allowed to go to school because they will be too educated and ask questions! I find it hard to listen to women who say that their deepest hope is that their children will be educated, who themselves have very few rights. Lord, help me to know how to pray and what to pray for; help me to value this culture, as it is part of Your design. Forgive me for the times I have judged people within it. Help me see it with Your eyes. Amen.

News from Mike and Laura 24 June 2008

It has been quite a while since we last wrote to you all. A lot has happened to us since and we write to you all from different parts of the globe; Mike and the children are in Uganda and I am in Mongolia. It has been both an exciting and a challenging time and we could not have done it without God's provision and without your prayers and encouragement. A huge **thank you** for love and care and support.

It is hard to know how to see a country at times. One grows up with certain ideas and then there's also the Utopian 'sales pitch' aimed at tourists. Mongolia. The very word makes one think of somewhere you have to look up in the index of the atlas to find. You think of gers, Chingis Khaan and yaks. I wasn't really sure what to expect; research is research, reality is often very different. I have found it to be a land of contrasts and surprises!

Juuso and I have done a fair bit of flying together where he is supervising what I am doing, patiently teaching me the ropes of flying in Mongolia. We have had a fair few laughs! We have also seen a lot of things he has not seen in the 12 months he has been flying here. He keeps saying: "This has never happened before" or "I have never seen this before" and it has become something of a little joke between us. He speaks wonderful Mongolian and has a real enthusiasm for his work here in Mongolia.

We flew several times to a place called Erdenbulgan. It is a little 'happy valley village', "so remote that the 'evilness' hasn't reached it", cuddled up against an icy river that gurgles its way through tree-clad mountains. We land on a lush green field to an audience of fluffy goats and motorbikes. On opening the door one is hit by the scent; the field is a mass of grasses, tiny flowers and wild herbs which, combined, produce the most amazing 'aroma' and make us both instantly hungry! We drop the team off for the day and are escorted to a little wooden house nearby, where a lady makes us tea and lunch on her iron stove.

We eat minced meat covered in some sort of pastry that has been cooked in a steamer. Very yummy, too. Some men arrive and there is a little impromptu wrestling, some football and volleyball, and then we all hop into a van and head off into the hills. Mongolian people are very hospitable and very friendly. Our 'guide' is a Damjin Badam-Ochir, around 60. He is the project manager of Taimen Conservation Fund and shows us a small, turbine-fitted bridge/dam affair that the Danish government has sponsored. As the water runs through the turbines it generates electricity (only in the summer, as the river freezes in winter!!!) which was a first for the village. This in turn has reduced the rate at which trees are chopped down for firewood, which has helped to reduce the rate of erosion and deforestation. It is a breathtakingly beautiful nook of Mongolia, one which I am told is very rare. Tourists come here to fish! Imagine it: standing for hours on end in a freezing river! Must be nuts... Anyhow, the fish are all thrown back in once caught. I couldn't help but smile to myself at the thought of Mr Fish getting cross with himself for having fallen for THAT old trick YET again! Do the holes from the hook close over? If not, the river has a lot of holy fish. It was an incredible afternoon of exploring, question-asking and trying to get to know a little of the heart and soul of Mongolia. Damjin shared with me about the problems generated by the tourists; the local people receive no benefit from their coming and see them as just taking from their environment and not giving anything back. We shared some ideas and things I had seen being done in that field whilst I was working in Namibia. The people are really so friendly, so please do pray that they too will benefit from the tourism to their area as there really isn't anything else at all. There is no church here and there are no known Christians. Anyone up for a challenge in chilly paradise?

"But for every 'yin' there is a 'yang'", people here would say. We would say that for every life without Christ there is the reality of life without real purpose. As in every country, here too, there are the darker sides of things. JCS (Joint Christian Services www.jcsintl.org) has a project here, run by a wonderful Christian man called John Koehler, under the name of **'Springs in the Desert'**. They have an outreach to the many prostitutes here in Mongolia. Many women and girls sell themselves, especially during the winter, simply for a warm place to sleep. There are many terrible testimonies from these ladies of how they have ended up in that situation. Here is one:

"International Children's Day is celebrated on June 1 around the world. The idea is to promote the welfare of children and in Mongolia family ties are traditionally strong. The irony today is that in the capital Ulaan Baatar many are rejected or neglected by their family because of alcoholism, poverty or some social ill.

"Amongst those attending was Urna, 35, who is deaf and unemployed. For the last seven years she has worked at the Ulaan Baatar Hotel selling herself to men. The only problem was she hated it, she almost never got paid, she was beaten, abused, forced to take drugs...

"But at children's day she decided she wouldn't return to the UB Hotel again and threw her makeup away. Now she meets weekly with Alimaa from Streams in the Desert (a JCS partner ministry which outreaches to prostitutes) to read and pray. And she's ready to start a new life.

"Unfortunately for Urna she's met bad people all her life who abused her deafness and inability to speak. Her story is heartbreaking. It's sad to see how vicious and cruel people were; a policeman who turned his back as 10 men attacked her and stripped her naked and doctors who refused to treat her. Thankfully she has now found people that care and are trying to help her."

John is praying for the finances to rent a larger building so as to be able to offer more girls and ladies somewhere to come if they really want to leave prostitution. He asks for prayer for this as the needs are vast and the resources limited. Their charity still has tacit support of the government; please earnestly pray that this continues. Please also pray for the girls and ladies; that they would really know total inner healing and peace as they learn to trust Christ for all things.

Last Monday (16 June), after three-and-a-half weeks of studying, paperwork, training and supervised flying, I launched off on my first 'all by myself' flight into the outer bits of Outer Mongolia. No Juuso (the permanent MAF pilot here). I had watched the smoke and dust trailing behind Aeroflot's Tupolev 154 taking-off for Moscow; he was on that aircraft, heading off to Finland for furlough.

Last November I'd been promised blue skies and hot weather. Hmmm. One-and-a-half hours into the flight and I was in cloud and rain and the aircraft was rapidly icing over. The outside temperature was well below zero; I had to get out quick and so I turned back for 'UB'

(Ulaan Bator) which, at 90 minutes' flying, was still the closest airfield. I had 9 Korean missionaries on board and it was with a heavy heart that I explained to them that they would not get to Khovd that day. Due to this, the Korean team spent their time working in UB; we trust that in this, too, the Lord had His plans.

The next day I was due to take a group of American missionaries to Ulaangom. The weather forecast was even worse than for the day before, with forecast icing conditions beyond the capabilities of the aircraft's icing protection systems. We never even left the ground...

Wednesday was a bit of a relief as I headed south into the **Gobi Desert,** where the air is both warmer and drier. Whew, no problems as I flew a group of men to a coal mine in the middle of nowhere! The airfield itself was 7500ft above sea-level! (My 'home town' of Shoreham-by-Sea in West Sussex is 7ft above sea-level!) We flew past vast, parched plains, majestic mountain ranges, lunar landscapes and dried-up rivers. And in the near distance, off the left wingtip, a sullen China, watching our progress in silence.

It is quite incredible; the place is almost empty! You fly and fly and there is absolutely nothing. Then, in an act of total defiance, every now and then you see a little, round, white ger clinging to the side of a mountain or huddled up alongside a riverbed somewhere, quietly betraying the presence of a people whose lives bear witness to their precarious truce with this harsh environment.

My hapless American missionaries finally made it to Ulaangom today! (20 June) They are with **'International School Project'**. Together we flew over large lakes and more mountains, swooping down on Ulaangom at around 1pm. We landed and they dashed off to a conference (2 days late!) with the regional governors. It was a full hour before I managed to get refuelled and parked for the next flight, simply due to the language barrier! My English-Mongolian dictionary is getting a good work-out! Many people still speak Russian so the few phrases of Russian I know are also getting dusted off.

Tomorbaatar, my translator, and I clambered into the back of some ancient, Soviet-built van and headed off into town. The hotel was modest; I found out that I was actually sharing a room with a stranger, but it turned out to be Puje, one of the ladies on the team, and we became good friends over the next 4 days. The interior was painted one shade lighter than a Soviet helicopter's 'cockpit green', which I am particularly fond of, so all was well! I dropped off my bags and went to explore. The town has that air of Soviet dilapidation about it so common to many parts of the former USSR. It even has the old star and sickle on some buildings. It is all very run-down and I wonder what people actually do here. People stop and stare as, firstly, this is not a tourist destination and, secondly, because there are no female pilots in Mongolia at all. I put my jacket on...

I found a museum. I had been stopped outside it by 2 over-friendly drunk men and decided it was well worth going in to! The very surprised doorman leapt to life as I appeared and led me off to meet a lady, who hunted for a key, dusted it off and let me in. A small collection of stuffed animals and wading birds standing on mirrors for effect and a few dozen faded photos of strangers, as well as a small but very interesting collection of silver bits and bobs used on horse saddles, etc. The lady was quite adamant that I look in the souvenir shop, whose contents consisted of 4 small, painted plaques (hastily dusted off using the curtain) and a few little booklets. She had to climb over the counter to get them (in stilettos!) as the key to the hatch didn't work. I helped hold her, because the counter wasn't secured and toppled back and forward quite alarmingly. I bought a plaque to remind me of the whole museum experience, which lasted around 20 minutes. I had met a really nice lady and had a good time!

Now, what does one do when you don't speak the language, you have 'done' the museum, the room is cold and has even colder 'hot' water (well, at least it has water!) and it is drizzling? Go get a coffee? Have a snooze? No, of course not! You go and visit a small lean-to that has the look of a hair salon! You then totally lose all sense and ask the lady, using sign language only, to TRIM your long hair. Now, I am quite convinced that most hairdressers secretly harbour a fantasy to one day cut off someone's long hair, so it was particularly insane of me to proceed with this plan of action. Anyhow, I tried to ignore the scum in the basin from the previous customer and concentrated my efforts on peering up at the sky through the hole in the roof above my head. Once my hair had been washed, the scissors came out, still covered in someone else's hair. They made a thwacking, as opposed to a snipping, sound. I smiled to myself as I thought of poor Mike and what his hair looked like after I had cut it for him; he has trimmed mine in the past with about as much success. The hairdressers had several 'goes' at it and gave it a bit of a dry, and I have to say it looks great. She was ever so friendly and chatted away (it's a hairdresser thing, to be sure); we swapped smiles and she laughed at my 5 words of Mongolian. That was enough excitement for one day, so I decided to retreat to the room and take an arctic shower...

It was a cold night. I snuggled down deep beneath the 2 duvets and slept soundly until 6am. "Did you hear the disco last night?" I was asked at breakfast by several bleary-eyed team members. Disco, what disco? The really funny part is that it is right next to my room! Praise the Lord for a mother who let 'baby Laura' learn to sleep amidst noise! The team gathered for breakfast; bread and marge, a boiled egg and a bowl of 'koosh' (a bit like Kreemy Meal porridge!) all washed down with black tea. Everyone was chatty and in high spirits, ready for the day's teaching seminars.

It is an interesting group. One Mongolian lady, Olya, came to the Lord around '93 and went off to the Philippines to study Theology for two-and-a-half years and is now in full-time ministry. Another 3 ladies in the group are all involved in various Christian NGOs, also all Christians since the early 90. There was Puje and Tuya, both translators, and Mrs Tsemple, an elderly lady who does a lot of mentoring and has helped many of the leaders in Mongolia come to the Lord. They join the Americans here and make up the Mongolian half of the team. Three American men and one American lady make up the other half. The Americans are all 50+ and have all been, or still are, in the teaching profession back in the States. The team is here running courses on leadership for the local leaders. They are not 'allowed' to teach the Bible directly, but all their leadership training is Biblically-based. The 100 delegates had assumed that the leadership training would endorse 'being in charge' and insist that things were done 'their way', so they were amazed to discover the concept of the **'servant leader'**. Puje, one of the ladies on the team, told me how well it had gone down. One man, the city's welfare officer, was seen to serve others tea, etc. during a break, and how surprised and challenged all the delegates were at this approach to leadership. Christianity is not much appreciated here, mostly because it is seen to be autocratic and domineering. These delegates have been introduced to Christianity in action! Please do pray for Church leaders, missionaries and others here who are Christians; that we may hold on to the attitudes and thoughts that God has asked of us and that we do not spread the idea that we are autocratic and domineering. Buddhism is very popular and it has strong teachings on love in action; Christians have a real challenge trying to show where our love in action is different.

All major cities in Mongolia have now at least one church, which is actually quite amazing when you realise how vast the country is and just how incredibly isolated these places are. Less than 1% are believers, though.

Once the team was done with its work we all headed off to Ovs Lake. There was much chatter in the little, Russian-built bus and we were all in high spirits as we bounced and jostled about, Mongolian folk music mixing in with our din.

The plains are vast in the extreme. So vast and open that you manage to lose and find yourself all in the same moment. You stand amidst this huge expanse so small and unimportant, and then you remember that the One who created all this sees you standing in that very spot and knows your name! You drive and drive and seem to never progress any further along it, this huge grassy plain surrounded by towering, granite mountains. And then, of course (!), we came upon a caravan of camels! A nomadic family was on the move; around 20 camels and 8 people, their gers packed up on the backs of the camels, their little baby tucked up into a side-saddle. We shook hands and shared smiles and jabbered away, hands pointing and painting pictures as we tried to communicate. The people were so open, so friendly, and so calm, the gentle owners of calloused hands that held the well-worn tethers with care and skill, wind-chapped faces, broad smiles and open hearts. Naturally, we all got to sit on the back of a camel and have our photo taken. And then they were off. Having already completed 200km they were moving on to find summer pasture for their camels. And so we watched them plod off into the distance, a low murmur of hooves and voices melting into the landscape as the vastness quickly absorbed them into itself.

The Ovs Lake, 86km from one end to the other, is a protected area; families and backpackers come here to swim and wade and generally relax. It is slightly saline and attracts a large number of endangered bird species. The space is so open and so quiet that our noise was quickly swallowed up; you find yourself naturally lapsing into silence and wandering off to explore and just relax. It was wonderful and beautiful beyond measure.

We dropped in on a family of herders living in a ger. It was quite late by now, 8pm, and the sun was still high in the sky. Their cows had all decided that it was time to come home and get milked and so we found ourselves in the midst of very real herder lifestyle! Around 25 people from one extended family share this area; they all came to see what was going on. Smiling children, prancing horses, lowing cows and over-excited dogs all joined in the fun. We were invited in for bread and boiled milk - Mongolian people always treat total strangers in this way,

I was told. How amazing! These people did not own a camera and were thrilled when the team leader offered to take a family portrait (he printed the photos off that night and sent them on to the family the next day!) and I have to say it was a really happy and contented group of people that stood there to have its photo taken.

We drove back to Ulaangom via a different route, one that took us up through a high, mountain pass. We passed Buddhist shrines and piles of rocks (part of the Ovoo religion; you throw a rock on the pile, walk around it and make a wish for safe travel) and were reminded of the reality of the lives of most here; shepherds without The Shepherd. As we slid down into the valley, Ulaangom drew closer and the scene became a little dimmer, a little darker. The contrast between the 'nomadic idyll' and the city could not be greater! Dilapidated buildings, many sporting brightly-coloured political flags that look like trapped butterflies in an old web, crumble quietly alongside slabless pavements and broken roads. I wonder at the dreams of their inhabitants, of the hopes and aspirations of their youth and their young. The town is, like all others in Mongolia, isolated and has high unemployment. Many families are separated as the father has moved to UB or another country in search of work.

We were all up and away very early the next day, heading off to Khovd in the far west of Mongolia. Here the team was meeting with a group of 27 leaders. Two Mongolian ladies who live in Khovd are managing this leadership-mentoring project and the International School Project team was coming to see how they were doing, to encourage them and to meet their group. Fifteen of the 27 local leaders have come to the Lord in the last few years! This all due to a 'silent' witness of lives simply lived out in the Christian way, of questions answered and love given.

I remember well when Christians in the UK were asked in the late 90s to pray for and fund an aircraft for Mongolia. MAF supporters responded with enthusiasm, so enabling the aptly named 'Millennium Messenger' to go into action in 2000. All I can tell you is that **countless lives have been reached and touched by this aircraft and the people we fly in it.**

And whilst I am gallivanting around Mongolia, Mike and the children are in Uganda. Many, many thanks for your prayers for our family. It is really tough being apart and Mike has had to deal with both children taking turns at being ill with a fever that is doing the rounds at school. Quite a few sleepless nights for him! Mike is really enjoying his work with MAF Uganda's **puppet ministry** (Out of the Blue) and they are all preparing for an outreach trip with Sam Tsapwe of Jesus Film Ministry. Please do pray for the whole team as they practise; that they will know how to reach people within their cultural context, for safe travels to and fro and for opportunities to witness to many in this unique way.

Prayers of praise and thanks for our safety, my successful training, the children's continued happiness and Mike's incredible steadfastness and wisdom as a **single dad**. And thank you to you all for your support. We value and appreciate your prayers and encouragement and, at this time of world financial crisis, we don't take your financial support for granted, knowing that it is sacrificial for you. We pray that each one of you will be blessed beyond measure.

"How beautiful on the mountains are the feet of those who bring good news, who proclaim peace, who bring good tidings, who proclaim salvation, who say 'Our God reigns'." Isaiah 52:7.

With much love and thanks, Mike, Deborah, Ivan and Laura.

Lord, You have given me an amazing husband! His heart is so big, he is so gentle and so jolly patient! He has brought the best out of D&I and he has supported me through so much this year. He has valiantly cared for the children alone for weeks on end, through their illnesses, school crises, friend crises and all the rest! Thank You for the blessing he is to me! Thank You for D&I, for all that they bring into my life. Lord, please care for my family whilst I am away. Please bring me back safely; help me make all the right decisions as I fly in the hostile weather environment of Mongolia.

Thank You for this time in Mongolia, for all that I am seeing, for all that I am experiencing. Lord, so many have not even heard of You! Buddhism, Shamanism, Atheism - no real perceived need for You, no real understanding or knowledge of You here. Lord, let the gentle breeze of Your Spirit flow through this place; let Your name be known. Bring Your light, the Light of Life, to this place. Protect and bless Your Church here, nurture her and guide her. Amen.

Dear Friends and Family: 2 July 2008

It is early in the morning here and the streets are peaceful once again. Please pray that this continues.

Elections were held on Sunday, the results disputed, which led to riots in UB yesterday. The President has declared a State of Emergency. Our office is very close (around 300m) to Sukhbaatar Square, so please pray for us today as we go to work. Pray especially for our Mongolian colleagues as these sorts of things are always more risky to the nationals.

The weather has been particularly bad. The flight on Saturday to Gobi Altai was very challenging and I was forced to turn back to UB. We tried again on Sunday when the weather was slightly better and completed the 6 hour and 48 minute return trip using all the specialized techniques MAF has taught me.

The flight to Tsagaan Nuur on Monday was also quite challenging as we battled rows of thunderstorms. I was unable to land at Tsagaan Nuur initially due to a sandstorm!!! By the time I had the passengers at their destination, a grass strip on the side of a mountain besieged by thunderstorms, it was 8pm (the sun sets late here!) I flew back to the nearest main airport and spent the night there, getting in to the hotel at 2145hrs. The good part of the 'delay' was that I had ample time at the airport to share with the 9 passengers who and what MAF is. Well, they asked! :0) They were mostly American and UK citizens who were going to ride horses. The end of their trip involves a horse race in which they compete against each other as well as Mongolians. This is used to raise money for conservation work. It was a fantastic opportunity to very indirectly share the love of God with these people. Please pray God will water these seeds He has planted.

I live on the 12th floor and the lift does not work, so the upside is I get exercise. As I was climbing to the top yesterday the Lord shared with me about how this is like our life in many ways. The view from the 12th floor is stunning. If the lift works, it is a great trip up. If not, you are so tired when you get to the top that the view has lost interest! Our faith allows us to live the life of grace God has planned for us; a bit like taking the lift to the top. A life lived where faith is a set of rules and regulations is a bit like climbing the stairs!

I have started to read 'Buddhism for Dummies' (aptly titled!!!) and am really quite amazed at what I am discovering. There is no God, there is no set belief system. "It promotes a set of techniques and practices that enables the follower to experience a deeper level of reality directly for themselves... The experience of awakening is the ultimate goal." The Dalai Lama says: "If you find teachings that suit you, apply them to your life as much as you can. If they don't suit you, just leave them be." Please pray for Mike and me as we learn about Buddhism, so that we can better share the Good News. Pray, too, for our, and the other missionary children here, that we will know best how to explain all of this to them.

My 12th-floor flat looks out over the back of an old circus. There are a few animals still there: a bear whose cage is big enough to do 3 paces in and then turn around again; 2 wolves whose cages are so small that they cannot jump or walk, but only turn around and around. The Lord uses this to remind me daily of the cages that most people here are living in; cages of Buddhism, animism, atheism and Mormonism. Please do pray for the Church here in Mongolia; that she will grow and thrive, stay true and be exceedingly blessed with His power and wisdom. A Mongolian Christian friend says to pray, too, for pastors who want the position to serve, not for the status it affords.

Mike and the children are well. Suzanne, his mother, flew to Kalongo, northern Uganda, on Monday, and flies back to Kampala today. She went to visit the mission station there. Mike and the puppet team will be doing a 'show' at the local school on the 13th; please pray that God goes ahead and prepares these children to hear the Good News in this way, that many will respond to the invitation to have Christ in their lives.

Mike is also in deep prayer about restarting flying for MAF. Please pray for God's clear guidance in this area; I am very excited but we both know that it has to be God's timing and God's will.

Many thanks for your prayers; God honours each one and we cannot do without them. God uses you as the "wind beneath our wings" many times!

With our love and thanks, Mike, D&I and Laura. (Sorry, and kitty!)

Lord, the caged bear makes me think of all those in Mongolia who are in a cage just because they have not heard of You. Thank You for the work of MAF/Blue Sky here in Mongolia; please grow and protect this work and strengthen all the MAF/Blue Sky staff here. The riots just remind me of how dependent we are upon You for our protection and for peace. Please guard the democracy in Mongolia and guide those in power; keep them incorrupt and help them as they lead their country.

Thank You for family and friends; for those who love and care for us, who pray for us and support us through our challenges, our ups and our downs. Please lead Mike clearly and let him know exactly what it is You would have him do at this time.

Amen.

News from Mike and Laura: 4 August 2008

Somewhere along the line, someone (or something) disturbed a nest of African Honey Bees last week. Perhaps because they were so miffed and because it was so jolly hot, they headed off, *en masse*, to find the largest thing that they could annoy and so descended upon one of our Caravans whilst it was parked in Kotido, north-eastern Uganda. Someone once said that a butterfly's wings flapping in the Amazon led to a tsunami somewhere else. How right he was!

My colleague returned to the aircraft to find it already occupied by around 300 stowaways! Despite our placing all covers, etc. in their respective 'holes', the bees had managed to out-fox us mere mortals and sneak into the aircraft at the flap joint. They then flew up the inside of the wing into the aircraft cabin. Now African bees are known for their aggressive behaviour, so he used numerous careful methods to try and get rid of them. As these things go, he happened to have a certain government minister waiting to fly with him to Kampala. Time was ticking by; it was already past 4pm. Eventually the pilot managed to remove all the bees but, in the process, 2 of the doors were slightly damaged. Happily, all passengers and the pilot were left unstung and they eventually returned to Kajjansi.

But it doesn't end there. Around 10 days ago I found myself standing-in for Adrian, our Operations Manager, and Steve, our Programme Manager. I say "standing" as the only thing I was going to be flying for the next 2 weeks was a desk. It's a bit like being a fire-fighter, really, and here was my first blaze…

It was decided that the doors needed to be repaired and so we set about trying to fit a week's worth of flying in the Caravan in to our 2 small Cessnas. It looks so tame when I read it but, well, you could smell the smoke as our brains worked overtime! Dozens of passengers were involved in flights to and from 3 countries. Many had international connections. God certainly gave us the wisdom we needed! We managed to get all passengers where they needed to be. To add to the excitement, one flight on our other Caravan was unable to get through the weather to Sudan and had to return to Kampala, and so we had even more people to reshuffle. It was a great team effort involving the 2 Bookings Officers, Carole and Sarah, as well as Engineering. (We were simultaneously trying to source 2 replacement doors from Kenya, which involved dozens of phone calls and copious amounts of paperwork, in triplicate...)

But it doesn't end there. Can you imagine the look on the insurer's face when the claim stated "bee invasion damage"?!!! Better still, can you imagine the look on the minister's face, as well as the response from the Ugandan Civil Aviation Authority, when a cartoon somehow found its way into the leading newspaper a few days later showing the minister "running for his life", hotly pursued by a swarm of bees? I am told it even appeared on TV. Fires numbers 2 and 3...

Fire number 4 involves an illegally-erected cell-phone mast smack bang within the traffic pattern at Kajjansi. As MAF is the airfield owner we have to work hard to get this one sorted out before someone flies into it.

A whacking great big, shiny new silver 4x4 with special number plates arrives. Inferno all over it! The uniformed driver opens the doors and 2 (tailored) suited men step out, all smiles and dark glasses. They are both representing a prominent Muslim NGO and looking to work alongside MAF. I have prayed earnestly for wisdom and discernment as I take this meeting on behalf of Steve. I listen, share about how we work to serve Christ ("Please read our mission statement on the wall behind you.") and arrange for them to visit when Steve is back.

During a routine inspection Stan, one of MAF's very experienced engineers, saw something that didn't look right - a small bit of something that has somehow found its way into the engine. Number 6. This could seriously damage the engine - how grateful I am that it was found whilst the aircraft was safely on the ground and not as we were taking-off somewhere! It means the aircraft will be in the hangar longer; inconvenient, yes, a little more juggling, yes, but thank God for revealing it now.

I share this all with you to show how MAF is so much more than flying an aeroplane, and just how many people are involved doing so many different things. Thank you all for praying for MAF! Please pray for our leaders who often have very tough decisions to make. Praise God for dedicated engineers who find all those little things that many others would miss. Please pray for the spouses who support us as well as having their own areas of work, be it at home or elsewhere. Pray for the children who have to adapt to all of it.

Our 4-wheeled maroon blessing would not start the other day. Now Mike is very good at fixing cars (which anyone owning a Land Rover knows is an essential skill, preferably acquired prior to purchasing said type of 4x4), so he went to our 'dealer' to get a new 'bit'. Our mechanic is a Muslim. All over Kampala Mike and I see the growing influence of this religion. New buildings and malls with mini-mosques inside, schools, etc., many financed by Gaddafi. Muslim 'missionaries' of the 21st Century. Warid is a new mobile company; huge, from the Middle East. Celltel, another, has just become 'Zain', also from the Middle East. Many shops sport photos of the Aga Khan alongside the photo of the President, Mr Museveni. Our good friend, Sam Tsapwe, shared with us last week about how the Sesse Islands, part of Uganda, are being bought by the Chinese and by various Muslim groups. Ugandans are too afraid of the water to want to go over there and evangelise, so others do. There is a gradual conversion to Islam amongst the islanders. There seems to be a steady march towards Islam here on the mainland. Please pray for Uganda as a country, for the Christians here, for the work of MAF here.

Mike and the puppet team visited a boarding-school in our area one Sunday 4 weeks ago; please pray for this ministry! The team members had a wonderful time and were very encouraged by the warm reception that they were given. Mike's mum was still here and she introduced each song, having spent some time with the children the previous 2 Sundays, and arranged for the puppet team's visit. The children loved it and the team has been asked to come back again next term to minister to an even larger group of children! Please pray that these children would know Christ in a real and lasting way. The *New Vision* newspaper had an article in it a few weeks ago highlighting the plight of children at school. The article states that 43,000 children were sexually abused last year. Many of the teachers are HIV+ and so infect the children. There have also been scores of fires at boarding-schools; there is one locked gate and no fire exits, so many children have perished in these fires. Please pray for the many vulnerable children in Uganda. Pray, too, for their teachers; that unhealthy sexual desire will be replaced with a Godly love and care for these children.

There is always the excitement of flying to somewhere new. You wonder at what you will find, who you will meet, what it will be like. Your mind provides an image based upon a map, an airfield chart, word of mouth and weather. Behind me are 4 passengers and a few hundred kilograms of freight; everything from steel pipes to lentils. The first 45 minutes were familiar, skimming across lush green hills out towards the far west of Uganda. Low cloud and thick haze meant that we only saw Lake Albert once we were 5km from her. I had the Caravan trace the lake's shoreline, little fishing boats bobbing about like matchsticks on a grey mirror, huts tugging at her sides. Apart from the hills rising slightly, there was nothing to show the colonial line on my map that I crossed stating that I was now in the Congo. I called up ATC and was greeting by someone with an Indian accent; part of the UN peace-keeping team. I land and taxi in, surrounded by Russian-built helicopters in various states of serviceability. As soon as I stop I am surrounded by people. Folk from the MAF Congo team unloading the aircraft, a refueller, an official or two. Passengers join the mêlée. They all speak FRENCH!!! Now, I can say "hello", "yes" and "no" in French and that's about it! The paperwork from Kinshasa is wrong, I gather from all the pointing and stabbing gestures he makes at my official flight clearance. I find someone who speaks English and we sort it out; profuse apologies all round, even though we have used this paperwork without a problem before. As I taxi out for the return flight I notice, for the first time, the UN 'blue helmets' along each side of the runway, hiding in their camouflaged huts at each 200m or so, guns at the ready. Bunia is a dangerous place to be. Please pray for our MAF Uganda team as we do this new 'route' for our MAF Congo team colleagues. The team lives in Bunia, which is a pretty tough place to live. Please do pray for them all, especially the spouses and the children, for whom it is the toughest. The DRC makes Uganda look like California…

We have quite a few things on the horizon, the adoption of our 2 children being one of them. Please pray for us as we gather all the required paperwork. We praise and thank God for miraculously providing a UK-registered social worker who was able to visit us here in Uganda and write a report, as required by the Ugandan High Court. The next step is obtaining Interpol 'police' clearances... I am off to Mongolia on 27 September, returning on 28 October. Please pray for Mike as he remains behind with the children and pray, too, for the children as they return to school in 2 weeks' time. It will be hard on all of us to be apart again and we will all have our own unique challenges to face, especially Mike as 'single-dad'.

We were very blessed to be invited to attend an MAF family conference this past weekend. The MAF families from the Congo, as well as those of us based in Kampala, all gathered in Jinja (Uganda) for 4 days. A team from the USA came out to minister to us. We had a wonderful time of singing, Bible-study and fellowship with each other and with God. The children all went off for several hours each day with 4 ladies from the USA for their own activities, so that we had uninterrupted 'sessions'. One of the sessions was a teaching on 'burn-out'. We would like to share with you all the points we were taught that most frequently lead to burn-out, so that you will all better know what to pray for!

Most common causes of burn-out:

❖ Long-term culture shock. This occurs when, several years into the term, you realise that you will never have a real friend from your host-culture. (At times God does move in a miraculous way and provide a real friend, but this is not the norm.)

❖ Team conflict.

❖ Management style; the perception that those in HQ do not understand what it is really like for those in the 'field', especially when new procedures, manuals, etc. are imposed.

❖ Spiritual warfare. Satan specifically attacks marriages, children, and our extended families. Pray that we will find favour with God, that He will provide a hedge of protection around us, that our marriage will stay strong and that He will protect our families.

❖ Schooling of children.

❖ Feeling unappreciated.

❖ Totalitarianism: where the job becomes all-consuming.

❖ Hero-cult: where it is difficult to communicate honestly with home churches and supporters for fear that they will not understand, as you are somehow seen as different -missionaries are not super-human; concern over what to say, how to say it.

❖ Financial support: difficult to keep asking for money; difficulties revealing our struggles; feeling the need to 'sell' yourself as a missionary to ensure continued support.

Mike and I have been here in Uganda for 3 years this September. Many of you have walked this journey with us for the entire 3 years. Some of you have joined us more recently. We pray that all of you have seen God at work here in Uganda. We sincerely hope and pray that you, too, feel part of this ministry. We rejoice with you in what God has been able to do here through you and us. 2008 has been an incredibly tough year for us; we have had a lot of time apart, we have had several serious family issues back home, Deborah has been very unsettled this year, there have been many extra exams to take, the weather has been challenging in the extreme, the workload high on all fronts and our (especially for Mike!) parenting skills have been tested to the max. We ask you to please keep on praying for us and to please keep loving and caring for us. Thank you for all you have done to extend His Kingdom!

With our love and thanks, God bless,

Mike, Laura and D&I.

Lord, You kept me going, thank You! You promise to hold us up, to keep us from sinking, to give us wisdom and strength - I can testify that You have done all those things for me these last few weeks and I thank You and praise You for that. It has not been an easy time. Deborah has struggled with me being away for so long; help me to know how to reassure her. Give me the patience I need at this time.

Thank You for making it possible for us to start flying into the DRC. Lord, help us all as we adjust to new procedures, new officials and new routes. Let MAF Uganda find favour here so that we can really help MAF Congo multiply its mission here. Their work is so vital to the missionaries here; each flight is a real life- or time-saver. Please strengthen the MAF Congo team here; they live under very difficult circumstances and face many physical as well as personal challenges. Be especially close to their children, who are very isolated and cannot readily go out and about.

Thank You for our team in Uganda. I pray for our managers, especially our PM, Steve, with his huge workload. Hold them all in Your care.

Amen.

News from Mike and Laura: 18 September 2008

It is rumbling outside, huge drops are just starting to fall. The cat has caught a lizard so has been booted outside, much to her disgust, but no doubt to the relief of the hapless reptile. Deborah and Ivan should return from school in 20 minutes or so. And so life goes on. Today has been a test of faith as Mike and I try to get our hearts to agree with our heads that God's plans are always for our best and for His glory. Mongolia now appears slightly further away on the horizon than it did yesterday.

Mike went to visit the lawyer yesterday to check up on the progress being made towards our court hearing for adoption of D&I in November. There is a new judge on the bench! We had been told by various people within the system that we would be allowed to apply for early adoption as we have good grounds and have had the children for over two-and-a-half years. The new judge does not wish to follow this option and we will now have to wait until the end of April. Last week we heard about another requirement: he has also asked us to obtain another order which none of the MAF families here has heard about; so now we are all dashing about trying to obtain these. Some of the magistrates have told folk that they will only provide the piece of paper upon payment of around £100/child!

This decision leaves us with a few 'problems' to solve. Far too many to bore you with here but please do pray for grace and wisdom. It also leaves MAF Mongolia without a second pilot for at least another 10 months. The only pilot there, Juuso, really needs all our prayers for strength and wisdom as he continues to carry the flying load alone. The Mongolian Civil Aviation Authority has also placed a few new obstacles in the way which means that, at this stage, MAF cannot fly to most of the airstrips it services in Mongolia. Our being held back (unless some other Divine instruction to the contrary arises) will, no doubt, be a further frustration to our colleagues in Mongolia. Please do pray for the team there, for the missionaries whom we cannot now fly, and for wisdom for Paul Brookes as he leads the team. Please pray for us, as well, as we come to grips with this situation, trusting His ways and His timing. At this point, however, we would still like to kick the cat!!!

The start of this week saw me fly Far Reaching Ministries (FRM) to Kauda, via Nimule, both in Sudan. Vicky Bentley got off her USA flight and straight onto the Caravan. The weather was lovely, albeit those below us were enveloped in a warm and soggy blanket of early morning cloud. We flew for one-and-a-half hours to reach Nimule, Sudan. Vicky had quite the reception! FRM trains chaplains for the Sudanese People's Army and a flight of them stood smartly in line and to attention as she disembarked, greeting her enthusiastically. I press-ganged several of them into helping me load 750kg of Bibles (in Arabic), copies of 'Jesus loves you my Muslim friend' (also in Arabic), camel saddle-bags, chaplains' uniforms and building equipment. No need to feel guilty about not making gym today! We also picked up James, a Sudanese chaplain who has worked with Vicky and FRM for many years now. We waved goodbye and the 3 of us set off, clouds of dust in our wake, for just beyond North 11 degrees, a 3 hour and 12 minute flight.

I was struck, once again, by the sheer beauty of Africa. There is a certain 'thing' about the place that never fails to inspire and impress me. Huge rivers, vast areas of swamp, mountains, plains and a sky that somehow contains both an African blue, all of its own, as well as some of the most treacherous weather imaginable. I noted on the map as we crossed the Al Bahi al Abyad River heading toward the town of Al Ara ish. This was no longer 'Southern Sudan'...

We finally made Kauda, flying over the speck of a village that you will find nestled amongst the Nuba Mountains, to alert folk to our arrival, and over the strip, to make sure it was safe to land. We were about to touch down in what was once, for Christians, one of the most persecuted places on the planet. It was beautifully green and lush. The mountains proudly boast their green coats, which will vanish within a few weeks once the rains stop and the place, once again, promptly reverts into a baking-hot dust-bowl. We landed at 1430hrs. I noted a mosque at the end of the runway...

FRM have spent the last 6 months planning this. We were due to stay in the Norwegian Church Compound, a truck was due to come and collect the freight (and us!), and all was to be well and orderly. Hmmm. But then again, perhaps not. Dropping into a Muslim area in the middle of Ramadan with a bunch of Bibles is bound to stir up the enemy! We waited, and we waited some more. And then some more... The place was deserted as most folk were sleeping. During Ramadan people 'live' at night, eating and working. By day, they sleep and pray. At around 1730hrs James spotted a truck and dashed off to speak to the driver. He returned triumphant! It was not safe to unload the aircraft until we had a truck, so we now set about unloading the aircraft. One box broke open and 20 Bibles scattered themselves all over the place. The men jabbered away in Arabic and the only word I understood was 'Bible' - well, that they had heard of it was a good start!!! It was wonderful to see 2 men, both chaplains working out there someplace with FRM (part of the 'camel corps'; they each own a camel and go all over the place with the Gospel!!!) reading the Bibles and smiling!

The truck put around 400kg on the back and headed off into the rapidly approaching sunset. And never returned! What did come was the manager of the Norwegian Compound. A Muslim man. Being hungry and tired, I guess 2 females in trousers, drinking water in the middle of Ramadan was too much for him. (And, no, you cannot load 750kg and fly a Caravan in a skirt dehydrated.) "I am not happy to see you," he said. He had told the truck driver not to return, did not want us to stay at his compound and proceeded to be as difficult and unpleasant as possible. I was suddenly very happy I had brought my sleeping-bag! I mentioned to him that he should not worry, it was OK; we would be fine in the back of the aircraft and would find accommodation and a truck the next day. Vicky was her diplomatic best - and when you think she had been flying for 3 days, one really has to admire her! It being 1800hrs and nearing sunset, we set about loading the remaining 350kg back into the aircraft. He relented and said we could stay at the compound. So we smiled sweetly, offered profuse thanks and set off, on foot, to the compound. We arrived an hour later, just as it was getting dark, somewhat breathless as we had maintained quite a brisk pace to avoid being caught in the dark. We supped on *halawe* from Egypt, bread, fruit and local sweetmeats, nattered away the night and headed off to the *tukuls* (checked clear of snakes) at around 2300hrs. The only irritation was the numerous meals I provided to half of Sudan's tsetse flies. I awoke at 0530hrs to the singing of children as they walked to school; "something, something, Jesu…" – how wonderful!

FRM are setting up a 'base' there. Over the years they have trained up many chaplains who work within the Sudanese Army and cover all of Sudan. They even have folk from Darfur training with them at the moment. MAF will be doing several flights for them over the coming months as they send in supplies and teachers. Please do pray for the FRM folk; it is tough stuff that God is asking them to do. There is a group of folk here who wear the white Islamic clothing every day instead of just Fridays; they are from Saudi Arabia and belong to 'The Movement'; Muslim Missionaries. Things are quite difficult in Sudan at times so please pray for the FRM team's safety and for favour with those they meet and interact with. Pray, too, for the safety of all our flights to this area. It is a long way from home and we really do not need even a flat tyre!

Last Sunday Mike and the 'Out of the Blue Puppet Ministry (MAF) Team' headed off to a church in Kampala. The church is involved with several orphanages nearby and so many of the children (if not most) in the service were orphans. Mike tells of how he winced when the minister asked parents to keep their children under control. The puppet team was able to do a great puppet show for the congregation and it was very well received, especially by the children. The minister spoke of how Kampala has 275,000 orphans! But praise God that He is a Father to each one of us and that the puppet ministry can tell them about it! The puppet ministry is able to reach children in a special way, so please do pray for this ministry. Most of the children HAVE NEVER seen anything like it before! God has a special place in His heart for the fatherless, so please hold them up in prayer.

Today's newspaper writes about how children in north-eastern Uganda are being sold across the border for 2,500 Shillings - around 80p! They are being bought for their body parts. The streets of Kampala are slowly being lined by 18-month-old dirty, starving babies sitting on the kerb with their hands out, begging, mother a block away watching. Children here are very vulnerable indeed. D&I, sitting in the car as older children come up to the window, ask us many questions. We pray that God will give them compassionate hearts and us great wisdom as we react and explain to each window visit. We fly many aid workers and missionaries into these desperate areas: pray that God will become known in each corner, that hearts will be changed and lives restored.

Mike and I would like to thank you for praying for us so faithfully. God is answering prayers, perhaps not as we would have hoped Him to, but He knows best. Thank you for supporting us and for enabling the work of MAF to continue here and elsewhere. We fly to the Congo, Sudan and within Uganda each week - each flight is an answer to SOMEONE'S prayer somewhere.

May God bless you and your family with every good blessing!

"Cast your cares on the Lord and He will sustain you."

Psalm 55:22

With our love and thanks,

Mike, D&I and Laura. Oh, and one cat-in-hiding!

Lord, it is hard to trust You sometimes and even harder to accept that what we may want to happen may not. It is unsettling, to say the least, to be told we cannot apply for adoption at this time. "Why?" is a question that springs to mind but I choose to trust You and to believe that You have a plan that is perfect. I feel quite devastated, to put it mildly; both Mike and I are struggling with this, so please do support us and please do hold our hearts through this time. Thank You that You have placed D&I in our home and we know that You will protect that and we believe that nothing can pluck them from Your hand and from Your care.

I pray for the work way up in central Sudan; let Your fire sweep through that place! Strengthen those Christians there who are persecuted, equip each one to stand for You and to live for You and to show You to those around them.

I pray especially for FRM; protect their missionaries, grant them favour, guide them. Help them to show Jesus to the many Muslims living there, because You love us all and, in Your eyes, we are all equal. In Jesus' name, Amen.

News from Mike and Laura: November 2008

It has been rather quiet on the letter front of late! Life has been rather hectic and we have been 'sifted', as it were. We have had some really tough things to deal with of late. The good news is that the silver is a little further refined! (Zech 13:9) We have been challenged on all fronts; adoption proceedings, concerns over the health of family members abroad and uncertainty about our move to Mongolia. Your prayers have sustained us and helped us in ways You will never fully know. 2 Co 1:10-11.

As Christmas approaches, Mike and I want to send you our very best wishes. Your gift to us is year-round and you have helped MAF reach many folk and touch many lives by enabling us to safely fly hundreds of folk from A to B in Sudan, Congo, Uganda and Mongolia. Our most sincere prayer is that He pours out His blessings on each of you and your families, that you will be healthy and at peace, and that this Christmas will be an extra-special one for you all.

★★

The windows are without panes, made up of simple netting and shutters: all one needs in these climes. I look out through them, surveying what will be my new home for the next 6 days. I will spend this time with some of MAF's mission partners from ECS (Episcopal Church of Sudan) at their modest mission compound in the small town of Kajo Keji, Southern Sudan. It is less than 2 hours from Entebbe by air. Most will travel by 'coach', bus, truck, etc., a mere 18 hours at breakneck speed in unmaintained vehicles on unpaved roads. Many lives are lost this way each month. They are all subject to the whims of the various officials they will meet along the way. One says: "Sudan", and most will simply think of Darfur. However, Sudan is a vast country and the entire south is on its knees. Decades of war in which north has subjugated south, tribe has fought tribe and disease and poverty have ensured progress was non-existent, leaves one in no doubt that this beautiful area inhabited by wonderful people is a place in crisis. One is also aware that it is a small fraction of what is 'out' there. Most folk fled the area years ago and many have only recently returned, most within the last 2 years and several I met within the last 5 months.

At 1430hrs the heat of the day is peaking. Chicks and hen cluck and twitter quietly to each other, scratching through the tufts of long grass in search of grubs. Long, swaying grasses, magnificent mango trees and bright coral trees provide welcome shade, drawing many of the day's weary workers, goats and cows. A sapling is growing from the one wall of a seemingly derelict building: it is in fact a makeshift dormitory for schoolboys. Little mud huts, *tukuls*, provide the housing for the rest of the students. They make their homes themselves; following students repair them in turn.

That night, Anthony drives me to 'his' plot of family land. There, embraced by the long arms of the low Kimo Hills, is a large section of grassland surrounded by trees. We walk a little, cautiously as it is almost dark, and come across the foundations of what once was his home. We stand there and look; him into the far distance of his memory where he recalls his father and mother bringing him up there; the seasons, the people, the animals, the wars, the escape to Uganda - all drifting through his memory as he shares a little of his life. I look with eyes of the present; a mind trying to imagine what it was like, what it is like now and what the future of Sudan holds for these people.

Every single building, thatched or brick, that was not 'occupied' by the Sudanese Army of the North during the 2 wars, was totally destroyed. There is NO electricity at all. There is NO running water. One cannot even drive to Juba, their capital, without having to go via Uganda. It is around 70 miles direct; it takes around 16 hours if all goes well. His last trip took 3 days as their car broke down, twice. It is not uncommon for people to be attacked by bandits *enroute*. As the Northern Army was Muslim, most of the Christian Churches were obliterated. People worship beneath makeshift huts or beneath trees. In response to this the Christian NGO, Samaritan's Purse (another of MAF's mission partners), has undertaken an extensive rebuilding programme. It is building 50 churches in this country alone.

The following day is a Saturday and we are going to the 'opening' of a new church. It is an all-day event. The little bus we travel in is packed full of joyful folk who are happy to have something to celebrate. Bright dresses, white 'church' dresses and vestments galore! At 10am the heat is still a gentle warmth, wrapping itself around rows of clothing stretched out along makeshift lines. Later, the heat will intensify, scorching them to a crisp. We arrive and the reception is tremendous; we all pour out of the bus and join the procession, banners and palm branches waving and home-made instruments playing, ladies singing and men drumming. The church itself is a modest affair but has been brightly decorated with scraps of material and Christmas decorations. A breeze tries valiantly to cool us, yet no amount of heat, discomfort and sweat will deter these folk from making the very best of this day and enjoying it to the full.

I meet Adam Lewis, the project manager for Samaritan's Purse. His dad was an MAF pilot in the Congo; Adam was born in Nankunde, so we chat about common things like aeroplanes and the trouble in the Congo. He is full of smiles and very calm about the speech he will have to make to 100+ people. Just as well because he will need to make 50 speeches for the 50 churches.

Bishop Anthony Poggo leads the dedication service. Rapturous applause and singing erupt as Adam formally hands the keys over to the Bishop. Folk are overwhelmed with joy at finally having a church to worship in!

By the time we leave the mud walls are gently hugging the last rays of sun, their happy orange glow also on the faces of those sitting outside, stoking fires to toast ears of corn. The Sudanese darkness advances quickly and quite suddenly it is the sharp black silhouettes of trees one sees against an indigo blue, faint traces of red clinging to the western horizon. In our bus there are happy voices and high spirits. People chatter away, each of us clutching our gifts of peanut paste, mats, hats and chickens. I feel very humbled by it all; how people with so little can be so resilient, how they find a deep joy in the simple things of life, how strong their faith is. Today I realise that Sudan and her people have stolen a little piece of my heart. Hmm, no, that would not be quite true; I have given it away...

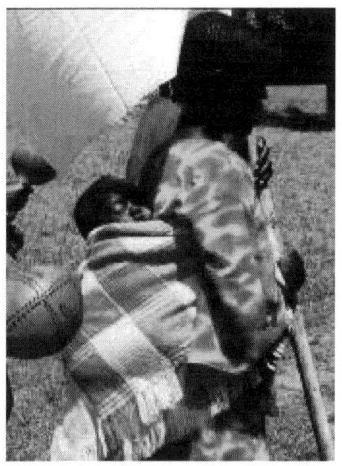

Our pantry-cum-cupboard in Kajo Keji.

Margret, a wonderful lady who did all the cooking and it was wonderful!

A family affair...

Processional drummer

Adam from Samaritan's Purse.

Man rejoicing, waving cow's tail.

We all ate after the service: 100+ folk fed!!!

Children at the opening.

Ladies celebrating.

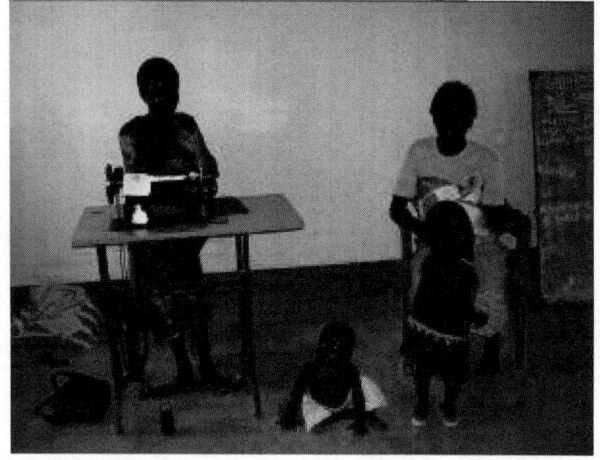

Landmine poster reflecting the realities of life here.

Ladies training at the Bethlehem sewing school. Grace, the lady who runs it, works totally on a voluntary basis. They have a constant struggle raising the funds to buy material, cotton, etc. The ladies, once trained, are able to earn a living and so build their families.

Rev Emmanuel and children at the ECS orphanage. They provide a home for around 100 children and babies. Bearing in mind that most folk here walk around with around 200 Shillings (about 7p) in their pockets, this is quite remarkable! There were both able-bodied and less able-bodied children here.

I visited a theological college under construction. Until recently the students have been studying in a makeshift lean-to in Arua, Uganda. The Episcopal Church of USA and CMS UK & Ireland have helped build this. We opened the new accommodation block.

The College Principal standing next to the ruins of their old, destroyed college.

Home, sweet home.

Rev Edward took me to 'his' church on the top of the Kumi Hills. I met a wonderful group of people. The elder told me that I was the first white person to ever go up there. The Sunday-School teacher

asked for help with resources; we are busy collecting.

★★★

In our previous email Mike and I mentioned that we were told that we needed to obtain something called a Care Order. We are thrilled to report that this was granted to us today (17 November) and that we now have all the paperwork (that we know of; we think!!!) needed in order to go to the High Court in March of 2009. The children's social worker was very helpful; we were spared the 'financial negotiations' some of the other families have been required to negotiate, simply paying the actual court and admin costs involved. We praise the Lord for all of this! They are doing well at school, especially in the reading department. We took the children to see Namirembe Cathedral a few weeks ago. They were baptized here when taken to the orphanage that the Anglican Church runs around the corner. It was very special to Mike and me, especially as a friend of ours from Uganda now works there. The nippers were quite puzzled but they will understand one day!

★★

Mike has been very involved helping Wayne and Bev of Cornerstone Foundation over the last few months. A huge, metal roof-truss fell on Wayne, narrowly missing his head, but striking and breaking his arm. Mike has been a patient and faithful taxi-driver and, given the traffic here, that is no small task! Their tractor had to be licensed; this took several days, the commissioning and purchase of an official Cornerstone stamp, many hours of patient waiting and then more spent correcting the incorrect information published on the relevant paperwork. It was tiring and frustrating for all concerned.

Plans had to be submitted for various sheds and buildings they want to erect in Kitgum. This is still being processed...

Mike and the puppet group are practising for several Christmas puppet shows. It is an exciting time for the group. Please do pray that the children will be blessed by it and that they will learn more about Jesus through it. Pray that the shows will go smoothly. No gremlins, please!

★★★★★★★★★★★★

Praise points:

- ❖ It has been a tough year for Mike; we have spent, in total, 5 months apart. Thank you all for your prayers for us as a family! PTL for good fathers!

- ❖ We have been kept safe on the roads and in the sky and have enjoyed good health for the majority of the time.

- ❖ God has enabled me to pass numerous courses and training programmes; it has been really challenging and quite stressful at times. We praise Him for His faithfulness and His goodness. I can assure you, it wasn't me!

- ❖ We have been privileged to see God working in many people's lives through the work of various missions and NGOs. It is greatly encouraging to see His Kingdom being built by and to get to know some of the wonderful people He is using.

- ❖ God has sustained us and given us a measure of peace in areas of great concern over family members' health. He has also protected our families.

- ❖ For our supporters; that they may know the value and impact of their support.

- ❖ Mike ran over the kitty the other day and she survived!!!!

Please pray for us in these areas:

❖ That we will have all the relevant paperwork for the adoption in 2009; that nothing else will crop up! That the Judge will see us as suitable parents and grant us adoption.

❖ That Deborah and Ivan will understand what is happening and in no way feel unwanted or inferior, but cherished and special instead.

❖ For Mike as he helps others, does homework with the kiddies and tries not to worry about me flying about.

❖ That we will hear clearly from the Lord with regard to Mongolia. A Canadian couple is moving there this November; please pray for them as they settle in.

❖ For continued safety here on the roads of Uganda. We both do a lot of driving and it is dangerous!

❖ That I will continue to make safe decisions whilst flying. I have found myself quite exhausted at times; pray that He will grant me new strength and energy each day.

❖ That kitty heals completely and can jump again; we have to lift her up now so it would be nice (for both parties!) if she were able to do it herself again!

Lord, so much uncertainty if I look through my eyes BUT thank You that I can trust You and that I know You will work it all out as You know is best. Thank You that there is someone who can go to Mongolia in our place; please help them as they settle down there and learn the language, deal with the flying and blend into their new culture.

Thank You for my time in Kajo; You showed me so much and I met so many wonderful people. Your people! It was amazing and encouraging and eye-opening all at the same time.

Thank You for my family; we have a home, food, health, education - just so much. Lord, You have blessed us; thank You.

I pray for our many supporters, for our friends and family. We wouldn't be here without You and we would struggle to stay here without them and their prayer and cares. This Christmas, please reassure them of Your love for them; let them know that You delight in them, that their service to You is a pleasing sacrifice.

Amen.

Merry Christmas and God bless!

A little news:
December 2008

It will be our fourth Christmas here in Uganda. The power is just back so the fan is on full blast as it is hot and sticky tonight. I can only stand back in amazement as I reflect on the changes in our lives since that first Christmas in Uganda. Hot and sticky with power cuts are about all that is the same! Our 'study' now has a little 5-year-old snoring away quietly, the bed littered with teddy and toys. The 'spare room' now has a 5-year-old example of perpetual motion with pink frills tossing and turning under her mosquito net. We have a Christmas tree with all the decorations bunched up at around waist height and a host of toilet-roll angels poking out from under the tinsel. I can now cook minus the black bits (well, 99% of the time!) and I have just made my first gingerbread house for the little darlings. (Does one actually keep it or eat it?!) I shall skip the grey hair and wrinkles bit... But God has been exceedingly gracious to us!

Our programme has changed. Families have gone, have come. We now do regular flights to the DRC and our Sudanese programme has expanded. Many of our mission partners have branched out into new areas and some have moved on, their work successfully completed. Plans to branch out into the Sesse Islands are well on their way to being fully realised. Today Mike and I joined a few others counting rivets et al in the hangar as part of the annual stock-take; plans are in the pipeline for an improved hangar area and possible sharing of facilities with another mission flying group. Our faithful Kajjansi staff are still there, adapting to new roles and demands as times and needs change. We await the arrival of a third Caravan; MAF is busy, God is busy!

December provides a welcome variety of child-focused events! This past Saturday Mike and the puppet team 'performed' at the 'Jesu Fest' (the Heritage International School Christmas Festival). The performances went extremely well! The team was thrilled to hear that Jacqueline, the team leader, had been approached by 3 different people asking them to come and perform for their groups. This unique Christian ministry is growing; please pray for the Wents as they lead the group, for the health of the group as they do many Christmas performances at this time of year and for those who hear and see; that many may hear the Good News and get to know He who is the 'reason for the season'.

It was a classic case of 'might is right'! It was the penultimate stop of the day where I was to pick up one passenger. I'd been flying for a good 8 hours on our Sudan shuttle and the aircraft was full. I'd been told about a VIP movement at Kajo Keji (the stop in question) but that it was fine to proceed there as they had moved on. We arrived overhead to find 2 massive, armed, military helicopters parked on the rather short, grass strip. I circled for several minutes, finally speaking with a pilot on the ground who told me that they would not be able to leave for another 30 minutes. We were sadly unable to wait and so had to leave our hapless passenger behind. There were a lot of "oh dear"s and "shame"s from the cabin!

The members of one of our mission partners, World Harvest Mission (we were flying extensively for them during the Ebola crisis this time last year!), based in Bundibugyio (western Uganda) have been praying about moving into Sudan for some time now. Believing the time to be right, a family has just moved to Mundri, Sudan! A short-term team of 4 folk had gone up with them and I picked them up last week, returning them to Entebbe for a flight back to the USA. It was wonderful to see them all say goodbye to each other: one could just see the friendship and love that had grown there. The family has children and they were especially cherished by the team. The Christian love and fellowship displayed in that farewell was a wonderful witness to the rest of the people on the aircraft! Please pray for this family as they settle in, especially for the children: it is 35°C-40°C during the day this time of year!

New Hope Uganda has sponsored a youngster through school here in Uganda. Moses Baguma, 16, dreams of being a pilot. New Hope contacted MAF and asked if we would let him spend some time with us, which MAF did. MAF's Ilonka Barendse took him under her wing and sorted out time for him in the office and hangar and then a day with me flying. Moses loved it! It was his first flight ever! He got to fly all over Uganda and see what MAF does. Please pray for him as he pursues this dream; that he will do well in his final 2 years at school as well as gain the right qualifications and the sponsorship he will need. Moses lost both parents many years ago. He has managed to track down a few of his siblings and is still searching for remaining family members.

Around a month ago I flew Dorie Helsey, a friend of a long-time missionary serving with Christian Vet Mission, to Moroto. Dorie's friend has been living in the Karamoja area for many years now. This lady is wonderfully special. She has been instrumental in setting up 'peace villages' in the area. The rival tribes literally battle each other for cattle; many die in these battles each year. Tribal feuds are just part of life here. Men from one tribe recently kidnapped and then murdered an elder from a rival tribe within one of the peace villages. The lady missionary set out to help catch the men who committed the crime; she has subsequently received many death threats. Dorie had felt led to come out from the States and take her friend on holiday as she was under immense strain and very tired. I saw this missionary last week; she looked totally refreshed and bursting with enthusiasm! Wow! Praise God for caring friends! Please pray for God's protection over her life and that she will have personal peace as well as see peace in the 'peace villages'.

Out in the far south-western corner of Uganda is Kisoro. The town lies in a deep valley, surrounded by crater-lakes and towering volcanoes, all, thankfully, extinct. This flight was one of those where I am so thankful I have been well-trained by MAF! The weather was foul and so I used the skills I'd been taught to execute a safe 'ridge crossing' as I flew over high mountains beneath layers of low cloud. I was picking up a group from MSF. The recent renewed fighting in the DRC has caused an influx of refugees across the border into Uganda, so this NGO is hard at work there. We taxied out for take-off; as we lined up, a flock of around 30 Crested Cranes landed on the runway. It was a beautiful sight and well worth the delay it caused as we had to stop and get rid of them all! Please pray for our team as most of the MSF folk are 'secular' and we hope and pray that we can witness to them through what we do and how we do it.

Kidepo is one of the most striking parts of Uganda. It is everything one imagines 'safari' Africa to be and last week was no exception. I landed to pick up a large group from the UN and noticed that the resident antelope were very skittish. The long grass hides all kinds of pussy cats, of the rather large and hungry variety, so I stood close by the aircraft with the doors closed just in case. My passengers duly arrived, all very excited and enthusiastic: had I seen the large pride of lions "just over there?" I really love my job!!!

Merry Christmas!

Much love, Mike, D&I and Laura. (& kitty!)

News from Mike and Laura: January 2009

Dear Friends and Family

Happy New Year! We sincerely hope and pray that you had a wonderful Christmas and that, as we all head off back to whatever it is we are doing, we are refreshed and ready!

On 18 December I flew a great group of people up to Mundri. They are all from the Episcopal church of Missouri and have been there many times. Their diocese is sort of 'twinned' with Lui, near Mundri. Their team leader, a chap I have flown up there before, was as enthusiastic as ever. Revd Robert Franken was taking seven others up with him. We flew Entebbe-Arua-Mundri. Our stop at Arua was as brief as possible; at the time the Ugandan Defence Force was launching attacks on Joseph Kony in the Congo (across the road, literally!) and it appears that it was using Arua as a launching pad for its helicopters.

I was really blessed to be with folk who were leaving the luxuries of the USA and electing to spend Christmas in Mundri, a hot and dusty outpost of Nowhere Important. I think that they may well have known the true spirit of Christmas! I asked what they were up to; this is a small snapshot!

- "In 2008 the Diocese of Missouri drilled three more deep wells, bringing the total to six. We plan on drilling three more in 2009, at $17,000 apiece.

- In late spring 2008, our grant from United Thank Offering for $19,200 was awarded, and is seeding the purchase and installation of one community grinding mill, and start-up costs for a pilot micro-economic project operated by the Mothers' Union. We anticipate this project will have a huge impact for the women of the Diocese of Lui.

- The Priest that the Missouri Diocese sponsored, Fr. Stephen Dokolo, has finished two years at Eden

Seminary, graduates with a Master's degree, and will return to Lui in December to teach.

"From December 15to January 8 another team of eight have travelled from the Diocese of Missouri to Lui. The missioners will pursue these primary objectives:

- a medical assessment to ascertain how we can contribute to health care in the diocese.

- assist in the set-up of the grinding mill operation, which we are helping to fund through a UTO grant.

- explore how we might establish parish-to-parish relationships between Missouri and Lui congregations.

- further establish infrastructure (buildings and technology) in Lui.

"The town of Lui and the diocese named after it lie north-west of Juba, the capital of Southern Sudan, and south-west of Rumbek, a regional centre. To get there, our team will fly into Kampala, Uganda, on commercial airlines, and then fly to the airstrip nearest to Lui, in nearby Mundri, via MAF, the Missionary Air Fellowship. Lui does not show up by name on Google Maps, but Mundri does. The River Yei is an obvious landmark, as is the landing strip just east of the river. Notice that it crosses the road. Then the Amadi Junction is a bit to the north-east from there. Follow the south-east fork to find Lui."

MAF C208 in Juba, Sudan.

Later that flight I flew a man to Yambio, in the far south-west of Sudan. It is a 'hot spot' at the moment due to the bombing of Kony and he was coming home to be with his family at Christmas. Please do pray for those in that area. I then flew a lady and her two children to Juba, about an hour's flight due east. The flight was listed as a 'medevac' as one of the children had a serious eye infection and needed treatment in Juba, there being no facilities of that nature in Yambio.

On 23 December I was in Yambio again, this time picking up a team of 4. They had been setting up a Christian radio station and training folk to run it. When I asked Revd Donald Warren what they 'do', this is what I discovered:

They seek to assist the struggling and persecuted church in developing countries, to give a hand up and not a hand out, to work themselves out of a job by training and equipping others in the Church to be everything God has asked them to be. They then move on to other mission fields. And below, one can see what they face once they get off the MAF aircraft!!! (Mike says that they should have used a Land Rover!!!)

I also flew Pastor J. Williams of New Directions International. They have many outreaches all over the world, one being in Yei, Sudan where they are "initiating an agricultural development project to supply food to southern Sudan." This is what he had to say about Christmas:

"Mary found her highest purpose being fulfilled in life by fully surrendering to God's will. I love her response: **'I am the Lord's servant,' Mary answered, 'May it be to me as you have said' (1:38)** I love it! Her response was not one of reluctance or resistance. She humbly bowed before the mystery of God's will. She assumed the only role that God can bless – that of a *servant*. A servant exists for one purpose: to do the will of his or her master. Mary found her highest and most holy purpose by being a *servant*. Remember: the only way God can totally fulfil His promises in our life is for us to humbly say with Mary: 'Lord, may it be to me as you have said'. Or as other translations say: 'Lord, be it unto me according to

Your word!' That's the spirit that made Christmas possible. And if you want to experience the true meaning of Christmas, pray that prayer that Mary prayed."

I was very challenged and encouraged by these words. It is my New Year's resolution!

On 27 December I was privileged to fly a very special man and his 3 colleagues. Dr Taketo (Japanese) flew with us during December 2008; he was totally blown away by the enormous needs he met with at Morulem Hospital in Uganda. So moved was he that he chartered the Caravan and flew a huge amount of medicines and other medical supplies to the hospital and worked there for a time. This year he wanted to go back during his leave and help out again, and so we flew him and his friends up. We landed and he was greeted as family; with much love and joy. A

special gift to me was that the aircraft had space for the rest of my family to come along. Mike and I believe it is important for D&I to know what mummy and daddy are 'up to' here in Africa, so we were thrilled to be able to take them along. Our 4 quiet Japanese friends had their ears 'bashed' for the entire 1 hour and 12 minutes' flying, mind you, as D&I were thrilled to have a new, tightly-seat-belted audience all to themselves!!! Happily, Dr Taketo likes children!!!

On the family front, we had a great Christmas! We missed our families ever so much but God is so gracious; we have been blessed with friends here and a wonderful church. D&I were in the 'play', Deborah being an angel. I have to say, she really looked the part!!! Ivan got to be a sheep. "Baa, baa…"

Mike and Out of the Blue Puppet Ministries were busy and had a great time doing numerous shows. Writes Mike: "The team was invited to a Filipino Christmas party. This was one of our first shows to a mostly non-Christian audience. We were very well received and were able to share about the real meaning of Christmas". The team restarts on 2 February.

Mike and I climbed onto the roof of the MAF Office (don't worry, it has stairs going up there…) last night and watched the fireworks over Kampala as midnight struck. I am flying tomorrow so it is all back to normal, whatever that may be. We hope this finds you all well and rested as you, too, go back to 'normal', and we look forward to sharing 2009 with you.

With much love and thanks,

Mike, Laura, D&I and kitty.

**Presentation from ATC Entebbe for training we
did for them.**

With Barnaby Bear...

*Lord, thank You for those who dig wells, those who set up radio
stations and those who fly from all corners of the globe to help their
fellow beings. Thank You for those who stay behind and are*

prepared to stay rather than go. Where would we be without them? How could we do this, cope with what we see and deal with the many challenges we face, were they not there holding us aloft in prayer? I think of the dozens of people who will pray for Mike, the children and me today. Of those who will pray for MAF and other missions, as well as for other missionaries. Lord, it is marvellous, Your ways are marvellous! Thank You for Your body, the church, that we can be a part of it and that we can all be blessed just by doing whatever little bit it is You ask of us. Grant us contentment with what You have called us to do, that we won't be tempted to wish it were something else or be somehow dissatisfied with the bit You give. Help us to understand the value there is in serving well where You have called us to be, whether at 'home' or elsewhere.

Lord we, as a family, face many challenges this coming year; grant us strength, wisdom and patience. MAF, as a family, too, faces many challenges. Please grant her favour with You and with man. As economies tumble, help us to trust in You to meet all our needs as an organization. Bless each flight; help each one of us to make it as effective as possible. Grant great wisdom to all managers and leaders within MAF and other missions at this time, as they face tough decisions and have to look to You for the wisdom to balance the many needs. Help them keep their eyes on You and help them trust You as You lead them.

I pray for all MAF's supporters, that You will bless them at this time. Honour their prayers, meet their needs, protect their families, homes and jobs.

Amen.

Dear Friends and Family:
19 January 2009

Sometimes it is hard to believe, hard to take in, hard to accept. Can people be so cruel, so unkind? How do others survive such terrible ordeals, raise a family against all the odds and still dare to hope?

My flights from Uganda to Yambio, Sudan, take me over the north-eastern part of the DRC. It has been a busy military operations arena of late; a Ugandan MiG-21 has reportedly been shot down here recently, the pilot tragically lost. On this route I fly over a town called Faradje. On Christmas Day the LRA attacked this small town, massacring dozens of people and abducting many children.

"Honore Tadri, 20, was in Faradje on Christmas Day when about 150 armed men surrounded the market square where most of the Congolese town's residents had gathered for a festive concert. The fighters, members of Ugandan rebel group the Lord's Resistance Army (LRA), waited for church services to end then slaughtered at least 143 people, crushing skulls with axes and wooden bats. When night fell they set fire to about 940 houses to help them see during a looting spree that went on until they left at dawn, taking with them 160 children as sex slaves and soldiers. Tadri hid during the initial attack but was captured in the morning and made to carry the pillaged contents of his neighbours' homes. He was tied together with 12 others and told to march through the bush. When their pace lagged, they were forced to kill one of their group, a man he knew. 'He was older than the rest of us. They handed out whips... We beat him to death. They forced us to do that,' Tadri said. The LRA has hacked, beaten to death, or burned alive at least 620 villagers in Democratic Republic of Congo, amid a struggling multinational offensive against the rebel group, according to New York-based Human Rights Watch." *The Daily Monitor.*

"I will communicate with Museveni through the holy spirits and not through the telephone." Joseph Kony, pictured right. Please pray that God will do something that will remove this man from his present position. He is mad, evil and possessed.

I do not even want to imagine what it must be like to live like this. Each day is a fight for survival: Will I eat? Will my child eat? I am sick; will I survive? Will 'they' come tonight? If so, will I survive? Will they take my children? Where can I hide? Will I be raped, see my loved ones murdered, have my hand or tongue or lips cut off? Will I cope with the new set of nightmares that will haunt me? Will it ever end?

I land at Yambio, Maridi, and Mundri and people talk of rebels in the area, of the roads being unsafe, of things being 'unsettled'. They tell me it is the waiting and the rumours - these things are the worst for them. I prudently alter my course next time to avoid flying over where the worst of it all is being reported. Those sitting behind me are either 'going home' or back onto the mission field. There is no course alteration for them. So green, so lush and so tranquil from above. How deceptive.

I think of those He has called to serve here; invisible nobodies serving invisible nobodies - both groups long-since forgotten by the worldly powers-that-be. Brutalized, traumatized victims of a tediously long and never-ending war, and Christians: both groups slightly uncomfortable to discuss over dinner. I think of the little nuns who run the hospital, hundreds of miles away from home. Of the missionaries and aid workers who are willing to stay. Of the teams I fly in who set up radio stations or hold 'eye clinics' for free. Of the Sudanese and Congolese mothers and fathers and children hoping for a normal life, many flying with MAF to go to Uganda to study or to receive medical treatment. Can a Caravan contain so precious a cargo?!

I drop off Oloo Vincent, the health Project Manager at Maridi. He works with Malteser International; I am flabbergasted to discover that Sudan still has a huge leprosy problem. Vincent works in the leprosy control and care programme. Vincent explains:

"Malteser International is conducting a leprosy control programme in three different locations in South Sudan: Rumbek, Yei, Maridi and Mundri. The region covers a catchment area of one million people. In Rumbek and Maridi, the organization has established a ward for the treatment of leprosy patients within the grounds of the public hospital. In Yei, the patients are treated in the hospital of Malteser International. Staff members reach out to the rural population with educational and awareness-raising campaigns. They also try to reduce the stigmatization of leprosy patients. Medical staff identify patients in rural areas and refer them to a health centre or hospital for diagnosis and treatment."

The population is also educated about leprosy, as folk believe many wild myths about leprosy and are stigmatized and shunned if they contract the disease. This means that they often go for treatment very late. Malteser also runs TB and HIV programmes.

Later on in the week I flew Amber and Terril Schrock of SIL to Kaabong, Uganda. They are involved in Bible translation in this area. The Bible in this people-group's own language!

"In Uganda, Wycliffe is presently working in four languages. These languages comprise over 860,000 speakers. What a potential there is for changed lives! The personnel involved in these projects are qualified nationals who are full of vision as to what can happen when the Bible is translated into their languages. They are using state of the art technology and are being equipped to do quality work as they are assisted by the linguistic, translation and literacy expertise of Wycliffe members."

A few days ago I flew a group from HART (Humanitarian Aid Relief Trust.) This British charity is headed by Baroness Cox. This remarkable lady has been working for and with the Sudanese and Ugandan people for over 30 years. She has visited many of the no-go areas during the various wars and has worked tirelessly to raise awareness and to source appropriate forms of aid for these and many other people across the globe. Please see www.hart-uk.org for more information on the amazing work this remarkable lady and her team are doing. The Baroness was visiting the Paorinher Centre in Pader, an orphanage she officially opened on 21 October 2007. Their key contact person or, as the Baroness calls her, "Our local heroine", is Christine Akot. These orphans are flourishing under her care; Christine and her team are placing these children with families in traditional surroundings, so deinstitutionalizing them and giving them a chance of normal life. A little more light in the darkness...

As a young girl I read about Helen Keller and I recall being suitably amazed. I couldn't imagine being blind, so I set myself the task of keeping my eyes closed for half an hour. It was odd; disorientating and very dark. I stubbed my toes a few times as I groped about but, half an hour later and with my curiosity satisfied, I simply opened my eyes. But imagine not being able to simply open your eyes. Imagine not being able to see at all. You start out seeing but then each day it grows a little dimmer; you see a little less and you yourself become a little more invisible. There is no political correctness' here: disabled is just that: dis-abled. A cataract, river blindness, malaria-induced blindness: you have no defence here in the third world; you simply wait to see what hand life will deal you. Eventually all is dark and you are another statistic, another victim of a perfectly preventable and treatable disease. But somewhere, someone has had a 'call'; He has called you to Christian Blind Mission. And you pluck up your courage and you go. Today you and your team are going to Rumbek, Sudan, a 3-hour flight from Entebbe; praise the Lord for MAF or else it would be a 3+-day drive.

I fly this team across mostly semi-arid areas. Towns are few and far between. The passengers peer out the window or doze. The dryness and harshness becomes more pronounced, the heat rises. As the land slopes downwards from Entebbe towards Sudan, gravity entices the Nile to wind her way from South to North through this vast country. Thin tendrils of green leak out from the edges of this watery serpent, quickly disappearing into the bareness. Hot and dusty little villages, muddy pearls spread out on an even muddier string, become defiant outposts of life, of hopes and dreams. People live as best they can; often very happy with their lives. Yet their dreams of an education, of something better for their children, mostly go unmet. An almost total lack of sanitation, garbage disposal, water and sewerage systems, hospitals and schools, combined with a defunct road system and years of war make this one of the neediest places in Africa.

I approach the little brown scar ahead that I will land upon, whilst they peer out at what will be 'home' for the next week.

Hands that will hold scalpels, which will deftly slice through eyeballs to remove cataracts (I feel faint at the thought of it!) or perform other such delicate operations, help unload the 600kg of equipment. The hot wind sends curtains of orange dust in waves. I marvel at this group who will work out here, bringing sight and treating many eye diseases. We shake hands and I am off. What will tomorrow bring…

As a family we are well; we went camping a couple of weekends ago and had a great time. D&I enjoyed their 'new chores' in the great outdoors. Their vocabulary now includes 'guy ropes' and 'tent pegs'. Toasting marshmallows was something of a highlight.

Mike has been busy visiting lawyers and the probation officer, collecting all the relevant documents and letters we will need for our court case. A British social worker came and visited us for the second time (3 hours!) and wrote a very favourable report. She was "thrilled to see that the children are so happy and so secure". Many thanks for all the prayers prayed; please uphold us and our family at this time. It is a tad stressful! We should get a date around the end of March to early April and will be sure to let you know once we do. And finally, from our PM, Steve Forsythe:

"Some interesting statistics for you: During 2008 MAF Uganda has flown over 600,000km (a distance equivalent to 48 times around the world!) and carried over 5,500 passengers (a 10% increase on 2007 and a 30% increase on 2006) and these passengers represent 349 different organisations and 3,306 individual bookings. This obviously would not have been possible without willing pilots, engineers, booking staff, handlers, flight followers, etc. However, a special thanks to those of you who are indirectly involved in keeping the aircraft in the air; cleaners keeping the premises tidy, cooks preparing endless meals, teas and coffees, car mechanics to keep us running around, logistics and administrative support, guards protecting our buildings, a finance team keeping the bills and salaries paid, airfield workers keeping Kajjansi operational, IT keeping the computers and network going, trainers running courses, those involved in prayer meetings, hospitality coordination… the list continues. Thank you to all of you."

Please do keep praying; we can't do it without you! Many thanks for all the Christmas cards, which arrived on 12 January; we are having an extended Festive Season here!!!

God bless! With our love and thanks,

Mike, D&I, Laura and Kitty.

Lord, thank You for hope. What I see each day is always a mixed bag. I see the terrible needs; poverty, illness, ignorance, oppression and spiritual starvation. Thousands of crushed spirits and broken bodies. I see broken minds and mutilated faces. Hungry children and hope-drained mothers. I can get so angry at times, wondering why it is allowed and when it will all end for them. Yet, each time I fly, I know Your answer to their prayers is sitting there behind me; each person, each bit of cargo - all answers to prayers. Thank You for the small changes I have seen over the years, for the slow improvement that there is, for the greater stability and the pockets of peace. Thank You for the privilege we as a family have of seeing these things, of growing up in these environs; we are stretched and challenged and, by Your grace, we grow. Lord, help us to keep our hearts aright before You. Amen.

News from Mike and Laura: March 2009

Out here on the equator we have the most spectacular thunderstorms! They are enormous and violent in a way that makes you realise just how small and insignificant you (and your aircraft) are. These storms often build up quite suddenly. The air is unexpectedly hotter and stickier than normal. The sky turns a foreboding shade of black; birds head off in search of somewhere safe to roost, those in the know 'batten down the hatches' and unplug anything they don't want fried by a lightning strike. You can just tell it is going to be nasty.

Last week at around 2am we had such a storm. My head managed to drag itself from sleep to almost awake rather slowly; I initially thought we were in the tent camping somewhere, due to the sound the rain was making on the plastic roofing. The curtains were all flying about, rain slashing itself through the netting on the windows, pools of water collecting in all the hollows of our uneven floor. The lightning was so spectacular and continuous you could imagine you were at a disco!

Eventually, the rain eased off, then stopped, crickets resumed their singing and the clouds cleared. Outside it was now a beautiful night. The moon spread out her silver mantle: all calm, all clean and fresh, all watered and nourished and ready for tomorrow.

D&I slept soundly through it all! Kitty just yawned and rolled over…

Of late, many of the NGOs we have flown, many of our friends and colleagues and, perhaps, even you, have been through storms. For our family, clouds are building on the horizon and plans are, well, not going to plan! After careful consideration MAF has concluded that a move to Mongolia would not be suited to us as a family at this stage. It is good to know we are cared for and that we work for a responsible NGO! Having said that, it has left us unsure of 'what next'. The storm is coming and yet we know that, after it, all will be restored and fresh for the new day.

What we do know (at this stage!) is that we go to the High Court on Wednesday, 18 March with the aim of finalizing the adoption of Deborah and Ivan. Please do pray for us all that day; that nothing will stop this in any way. We are planning a special 'Getting Our Parents' Name' party for them at 5pm on the day so do please also pray for that. We are still planning to leave Uganda at the end of May and return to the UK, where we will focus on arranging to have their Ugandan adoption recognised by the UK authorities. Beyond that we are not sure, but He knows and so we are in good hands.

Mike is mechanically gifted and very patient in finding and solving unknown mechanical problems! He has spent a good part of the last 2 weeks fixing 2 outboard engines on the MAF dinghy, based at Kajjansi. Mike took it for a successful test 'drive', but a second was needed in order to calculate the endurance that a full tank would give. So, last Saturday, we all climbed on board and got to see quite a bit of Lake Vic's islands. It was glorious! He is also busy building new props and stage bits for the puppet ministry team, of which he is a part.

D&I are doing well at school, although they are a little unsettled by their pending move. We have started to prepare them for life in a new country, so please do pray for them and for us (wisdom!) as we all get ready for this new chapter in our lives.

I have recently flown 2 trips for CBM. It has been immensely satisfying to hear and to see what this team is achieving. Its trip to Lado, Sudan, was a bit of an adventure for all of us!!! The runway there was totally unknown and in a terrible state. Samaritan's Purse managed to clear it (not an easy task getting folk to volunteer to hard labour at 45°C!) and provided me with as much info as possible. I explained Plan B to the team as we set off; if, following my detailed aerial inspection, the strip is deemed unsuitable, I would fly them to Kaduugli. They would then need to travel around 1 hour by car to their 'spot'. We stopped off at Juba to refuel, where I was briefed that if I did indeed land at Kaduugli I would be arrested. (This was due to my faith!) Plan C was born and Kauda was elected as a suitable alternative. God is good, so we needed neither B nor C as Lado was indeed suitable. We were greeted by an enthusiastic crowd of very hot and dusty Sudanese.

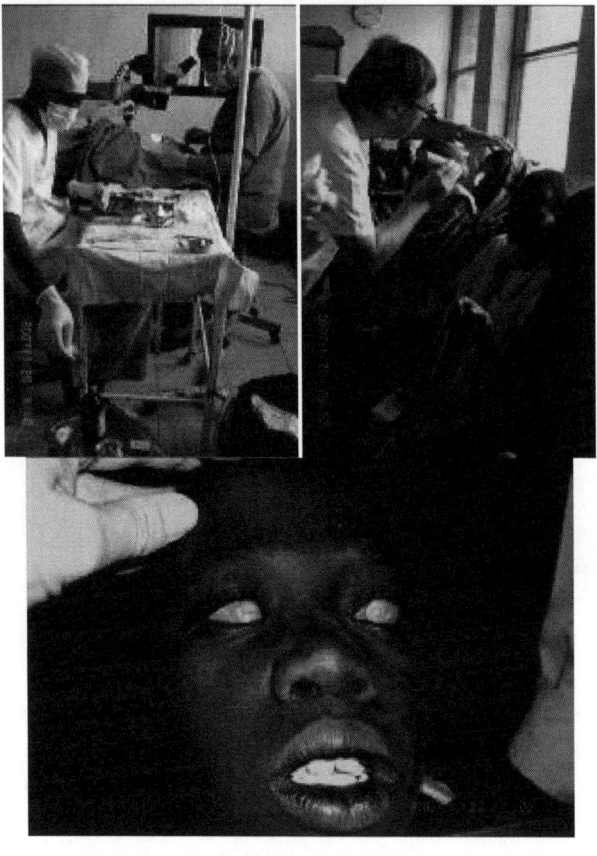

A week later I flew back to pick them up. I had overnighted at Juba on the way up. On the leg from Juba to Lado my stomach decided it had run out of goodwill. I needed the bathroom! My nearest alternative, Malakal, was at Security Level 4, with live shells littering the runway, the area having erupted into war the day before. I will spare you the gory details but suffice to say that solving the problem involved a little lateral thinking, a SicSac and the autopilot. I was exceedingly grateful that there were no passengers on this particular leg! Lado-Juba (two-and-a-half hours) went well, but the terminal area at Juba was 'no-go' due to the sudden change to who was in charge! I picked up Annie Russell, one of my bosses, and we flew to Entebbe (a further 2 hours). To those of you who prayed for us that day, THANKS! I made it all the way to the Entebbe loo, passengers blissfully unaware and un-alarmed! The CBM team saw over 300 people, performed over 180 operations, and emerged unscathed following 2 weeks in little tents with temperatures of 45°C, dust storms and strong winds. I stand in awe of them; they have been faithfully doing this ministry for years, bringing healing and sight to thousands. We will fly them up again next week - please do pray for these amazing people!

We pray that this finds you all well. Thank you all for your support; the work of MAF is not possible without what you do for her. God bless you and your families.

With our thanks and sincere love, Mike, D&I, kitty and Laura.

Lord, thank You that You never drop the ball. We may see times as 'uncertain' but they are not so to You.

Thank You for Your protection as we flew into Sudan this week; that the flight was unaffected by the sudden war, that we were unharmed and that You gave each team member the wisdom needed at the moment. I pray for the many missionaries who have had to be flown out, evacuated to safety, and so left behind many they care for and live alongside. Please enable them to quickly return. Thank You for the work of CBM; they bring sight in both body and spirit to many and work for weeks on end in such harsh conditions. Please continue to protect them. Thank You for hearing the many prayers prayed for our safety and thank You for answering them! Amen.

News from Mike and Laura: Easter 2009

Dear Friends and Family

It has been very interesting over the last few months, what with court cases, changes of plans and a busy home and flying schedule! So it was good to be away with ladies from our church on a weekend retreat. Four MAF ladies were in the group; Malaina, Ruth,

Jenny and me. The subject was 'talking to and hearing from God' and we all learnt how each of us personally communicated best with God. Mike and the other dads had to hold the fort back home!

One of the most outstanding things about MAF is its superb safety record. This is due, in good part, to the excellent maintenance teams we have. For this reason, many Diplomats and other such VIPs choose to fly MAF; we are, simply put, the safest.

MAF Uganda has flown quite a few interesting VIPs around so far this year. On Friday I flew the Danish Ambassador and her husband, along with several other members of the Danish Embassy and Parliament, to Gulu. I asked what they were to do there and was told that they were holding a seminar on Empowering Women. Women lead a life that is very different in many ways from what we would live in the UK. This is a secular seminar, but my prayer is that it will help rally and encourage the Church there to work hard on improving the rights of women. Catherine Ajok's story, as published in *The Daily Monitor*, puts this reality into focus. Catherine is the last of the Aboke Girls. Abducted on

10 October 1996 by the LRA, she has finally escaped. In many ways this is one of the harsh realities of life in Africa for thousands of women and children. Getting aid, counselling, education of rights, etc. to the people of Uganda is the remit of many of the NGOs and Christian Agencies that MAF Uganda flies.

"She was dressed in a light blue blouse with an orange striped skirt and red open shoes.

"She smiled as she spoke and held her baby boy. It was the first time she was away from the rebel camp, 13 years after she was captured. Catherine Ajok was one of the 30 girls abducted by the LRA rebels in October 1996 from St. Mary's College Aboke. She was the last to return home yesterday.

"'I'm very happy that I have returned back home. Thanks to the government of Uganda, most especially the UPDF', Ajok said. 'I can't say anything but I'm happy to be back home,' she added in an interview that Maj Kulayige ended shortly, when he stopped journalists from asking many questions that he said would traumatize her. One could almost say it was by a stroke of luck that Ajok got her freedom. She was pregnant, with Konya's child she says. When she gave birth, she was given to Col Binangi group because at that point, as a breast-feeding mother with a child during battle, she had become a security threat to the rebel leader. 'I had spent three months without seeing Kony,' she said at the time she was rescued. Ajok finally reached UPDF base after one month of wandering in the jungles of Congo since

UPDF gunships bombarded the group. She was in the western part in Doruma. The group she says was led by 'Col Binangi Swoop'. Ajok was found with her 21-month-old baby, Happy Odonga, whom she said was fathered by Joseph Kony and whom she calls her husband. 'We were over 30 wives of Kony. About 13 had given birth and the rest hadn't'. She was the only remaining Aboke abducted student in the hands of Kony who had made all the Aboke students his wives.

"Two of the Aboke girls died and she was the only one left. Rescued with her was a pregnant 15-year-old, Julien Merci, a Congolese.

"She, along with 149 girls, was abducted by the LRA rebels when the rebels attacked their school. The deputy headmistress of the college, Italian nun, Sister Rachele Fassera, went into the night in search of them. The rebels agreed to release all but 30 girls. The nun pleaded and offered herself in the girls' place. But the rebels refused and went off with the 30 captives. The Aboke abductions and Fassera's dramatic actions drew unprecedented, to that point, international attention to the insurgency in northern Uganda. Sr. Rachele and the parents of the remaining abducted children formed the Concerned Parents Association (CPA) to raise awareness of the abductions. In the course of their advocacy, the tale of the Aboke girls became one of the most widely known horror stories of the entire conflict." *The Daily Monitor*.

★★★

The following Saturday I flew on to Kajo Keji, South Sudan. I was picking up a group of Canadian volunteers, working as Alegent Health Clinic. They had been there for a week, providing medical assistance as well as training to those in the area. Bishop Poggo of the Anglican Communion writes:

"In addition to the attached, I would like to report that a Medical Mission team of 24 people from Covenant Presbyterian Church in Nebraska has been ministering in Kajo-Keji County for the last five days. This is the third time that this team is in Kajo-Keji. The team was invited by the KaETP with support from the Diocese of Kajo-Keji and the Kajo-Keji County authorities. "By yesterday, the medical mission had seen close to 3,000 patients. The team has not only been seeing patients but also has ministered through evangelism, water purification training, women seminars and trauma care workshops.

"Pray for the last day of this team today and pray for a safe trip as they return to the US this weekend.

Thanks

Anthony"

I am happy to report we gave them a safe flight!!! It was a great flight for me; the weather was superb, it was very early morning and we flew low down part of the River Nile and saw tons of hippos! Just a whole lot of fun and amazing beautiful; a whole plane-load of happy passengers, too!!!

It was also good to be doing a normal landing at Kajo! Three days before on my way in, with 12 minutes to run, I received word that there was shooting and fighting in the area and there was uncertainty as to the safety of the area. One of our flights had been turned back from the adjacent airstrip. My flight to Yambio earlier that morning had been conditional on the security there at the time; it was a day of constantly chasing-up security information, the operations team and flight followers chasing-up all possible leads. I overflew the area and decided that, given all the information to hand, it was safe to fly. A group of American International Team volunteers was somewhere nearby, awaiting my arrival. They had international flights that night. I landed, asked who was in charge of the group, and told him to help me get them all on ASAP and, very unceremoniously, 'threw' them into the back of the aircraft. Two trucks full of men arrived, no idea who, so I was taking no chances; 9

minutes later we were airborne, passengers briefed, bags on board, rushed good-byes. We landed at Entebbe and I explained myself to the rest of the team. I was forgiven for being so rude! :0) We so much rely on your prayers; for safety, for WISDOM that allows us to make those difficult choices, for favour with our passengers! With all that is happening in North Sudan, rumours about how long Western NGOs will be allowed to stay in Southern Sudan abound. The flights that we now do into Sudan are probably way more precious than we fully appreciate. So many are doing so much; please uphold these missionaries and NGOs and pray that they will all be allowed to stay and we will be allowed to continue flying here.

★★

We were all just about to leave the house on Sunday when the phone rang; it was Adrian: would I be willing to do a medevac? When? Like, um, NOW! A little boy, aged 3, was very ill. He had been in an out of consciousness, was having convulsions, and no one could really determine why. An hour later, the team having rallied round, I was airborne. I'd done my 'superwoman impersonation' and changed out of 'fancy Sunday frock' and into my uniform, Sylvester had come out to help me prepare the aircraft, Maurice had been on the phone to the military and the CAA and obtained the necessary security and flight clearances, Pam Lincoln had dashed home from church to do the flight-following on the HF radio, and Mike had been left holding the baby. Well, 2 kids, actually.

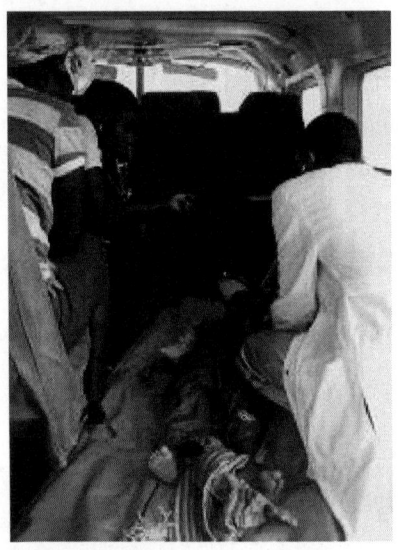

A doctor and a nurse accompanied me from the International Hospital of Kampala. We arrived at Matany, a dirt strip in the middle of the Karamajong. Curious people crowded around the aircraft and an anxious mother came forward, cradling little Timothy in her arms. We moved him into the aircraft, using the cabin as a makeshift ward, so that the doctor could examine him and they could ensure he was fit to fly. Timothy's little body convulsed and it was injections and drips and folk dashing back and forward trying to locate the correct medicines at their field hospital.

There are few things as heart-wrenching as being around a desperately-ill child, the mum looking on helplessly, chanting "Please God!" and hoping and praying that you are the answer to all her prayers.

Dark clouds started to pile up around and soon it started to rain, bringing fresh, cool air into the cabin. Just over an hour later we were airborne, navigating around thunderstorms, completing the distance in 1 hours and 12 minutes instead of the 16-hour drive by road. The ambulance was waiting on landing, and soon Timothy was off to hospital, his mother, Faith, praying desperately for his healing. A week later (yesterday!), I received a call from the doctor who flew with us. The boy is still very ill but out of a coma and managing to remain conscious. They suspect possible brain damage as a result of malaria.

So MAF is busy! All the pilots are zooming about here and elsewhere, folk are buzzing about in the hangars with hammers, in offices with phones and computers, in homes with nappies and trips to the doc to check that Little Johnnie's high temperature is not malaria, etc. Never a dull moment! Into all this please add 1 times adoption court case that goes, well, not as planned (by us, anyhow! :0)) and life becomes quite the roller-coaster ride! Mike and I were shocked to our core to be told "No". The Judge has, quite wisely, worked hard to make the adoption process more rigorous, following a spate of child sacrifice (up 800% according to one newspaper!) and an increase in child trafficking. We are working hard, together with our lawyers, to resolve these issues. We know and trust His plan and His timing. The initial reaction was not all it should have been, mind you, but thankfully He is forgiving! I drove into Kajjansi the other day and it was a glorious sunrise. Monkeys were playing on the runway, birds were happily flitting about, and we were all healthy: life is good!

One of the things that has kept us strong is knowing that so many folk are holding us up in prayer. We sincerely thank you for this: thank you for sharing the ups and the downs. We will be sure to contact you as soon as we have more news. Please do continue to pray for us, as well as for Mark and Sarah Newnham (he is an engineer here) as they find themselves in the same boat. We had our 'adoption party' for the children - a faith party!

So, we reach Easter with hope and great expectations of good things to come! After all, HE IS RISEN!!

Our love and prayers and all our thanks to each one of you. We wish you all a blessed Easter.

Love,

Mike, D&I, Kitty and Laura.

P.S. We think we may have a home for Kitty once we leave - an answer to prayer!!!

Lord, flying that little boy out has got to be one of the hardest flights I have ever done! To see his little body there, so small, so frail, in and out of consciousness, confused and helpless. His mother, distraught, people all around praying simply that he would survive. The weather was appalling, the doctor not sure of what was wrong and time was ticking by. It made me think of Ivan and Deborah and just how blessed we are to have healthy children. Once again it made me realize just how many people do not have the option of going to the doctor because there isn't one close by or because they cannot afford one.

Lord, thank You for MAF and that we could fly to such a remote part of Uganda so quickly, that You showed me the safe gaps through the weather, that we were able to get this little boy to Kampala quickly and safely. Thank You for those people who gave to make this flight possible, for those who prayed for our safety today, for Mike who cares for our children and that we, as a family, were all safe and healthy as we went to sleep tonight.

Lord, I lift this little boy to You tonight; please bring healing to his body. Hold his mother close to Your heart and strengthen her; honour her faith and hear her prayers.

Amen.

News from Mike and Laura: May 2009

Beyond my gritty burglar bars, years of dust and countless flecks of aging paint obscuring my view, a wall of cloud advances in tandem with the night. Birds circle in large flocks, the last few breaths of wind through their feathers before they roost for the night among the town's mango trees and cellphone masts. Below, oil-lamps are lit, enticing fireflies to glow and dance. Little fires are lit, braving the onset of darkness; their charcoals tremble and shudder and sparks dance into the air. Night traders fill the streets, their faces aglow as they look at passers-by with hopeful expectation. Chapattis, chicken kebabs, mandaazi, posho, grasshoppers, or dried fish, if you have the money.

The skyline betrays the soul of the town; new telecom masts sporting flashing red lights, old colonial rooftops slowly crumbling, shacks and lean-tos, all somehow linked and held together by a spider's-web of wires that bend themselves around mango and paw-paw trees and mostly do not work.

There are hardly any cars to disturb the night, just the chatter of folk starting their day (life here really starts at 7pm!!!) Then there would be the wail of the local Cleric as he calls Muslims to prayer, bicycle bells chiding dozy pedestrians out of the way and the screech of trucks slowly grinding their way through the gears as they negotiate the corner below.

It is Sunday and it looks like it will rain; well, it looks like torrential rain! The power has come on and the fan springs into life. We should have power from 7pm to7am providing lightning or some other disturbance does not snuff it out. I've moved here to the Mango Tree Hotel, having abandoned last night's digs ('The Tawali Hotel, run by Akhmed and co') in the hope of having fewer bed-guests tonight. I awoke this morning to find my head crawling with lice and my body covered in little bites. I made a lot of new friends whilst sleeping last night! I watch the eastern sky light up pink and yellow; the storm is ever closer. I hope my aircraft is safe; she will be busy tomorrow. Somehow I do not think there will be a film tonight as it will probably be rained out...

On Saturday I flew in Sam Tsapwe, his wife Sarah, and 4 others of Jesus Film Ministries. It will be a weekend of outreach and evangelism, our third to Lira in as many years. In that time a lot has changed. Our first visit was completed amidst much insecurity and we were basically surrounded by internally displaced peoples, their 'camp' covering most of the surrounding area. There was little sign of much to hope for back then. Today, food that has been locally produced is in the market, children are free to move about without fear of LRA abduction; people are able to return to their villages and farm. Progress is apparent everywhere. Today we split up and spoke at 2 different churches. The church I went to was vibrant and very alive! We all 'took turns' to speak and teach as this is what is expected. The service was from 10am to 2pm! I then took a small Sunday-school class, via interpreter! The children were excited to have a crayon and a bit of paper to draw on, a real luxury. But it will be the trip we did yesterday that will stay burnt upon my mind, as it was a reminder of where folk have come from and what it is they have endured. When you are living in a place, it is not always easy to see how things are changing. You get caught up in the doing of everyday life and, somehow, God's work and the progress He is enabling escape your attention. As we begin to face up to the reality that we will soon leave Uganda, yesterday was a powerful way of reminding us of what has really happened in the last 4 years. And much of this has only been possible because of the safe flight service offered by MAF to the many NGOs and missionaries working in these sorts of places.

It is always unsettling to stand upon a mass grave...

Saturday took us to Ogur, a village 23km out of Lira. The flight to Lira took 50 minutes; the drive would take just under 2 hours and the return trip slightly longer as it was far more entertaining. I think of the people we met, those who came out to meet us, singing their hearts out and dancing, clutching branches of whatever they could find, exuberantly waving them above their heads. Boundless joy at the sight of our small, rag-tag group of nobodies.

The sun already hot and high, we were ushered into a simple mud and thatch church filled with pastors who had come for the 'package'. One man had cycled 63km; the others had walked from miles around. Local villagers of all ages filled what space remained.

On 21 February 2004, whilst Mike and I were still preparing for work with MAF, Kony and his soldiers had entered this area. Back then it was a sprawling IDP camp, thousands of little huts crammed side by side, thousands of people displaced and dispossessed. On that day he set fire to the camp and slaughtered over 500 men, women and children, his sacrificial offering to the power of darkness that feeds his madness and controls his soul. When he left, the ground was drenched in blood and strewn with bodies. He just walked out and left them there.

A mass grave was dug and people were laid out side by side, in a circle, a community butchered and buried together. About half of the circle has concrete over it, which children play upon and cows cross. The other half remains unmarked save for the brick inscription at the circle's centre. The church stands as a symbol of hope here. I am asked to teach. What on earth can I possibly teach people who have survived this and still come out singing? I am just me, 1 of 8 billion, small and unimportant and struggling to keep back the tears. But then I remember, I am *here*, not just a pilot but His ambassador. I have a desperate desire to give something that will encourage, that will grow, strengthen and uplift them. And He is faithful and He gives me the words...

We leave very late, getting somewhat lost in the darkness, following what is basically a footpath in our mini-bus. Quite often it dies and we all get out and push it back into life in what somehow always is the uphill direction. Finally, somewhere near midnight, we run out of fuel around 2km outside Lira. A cyclist is dispatched to procure a few more litres and we wait, watching droves of drunken men stagger past us, fighting and shouting at themselves and everyone else. Finally the fuel arrives and, after another very long stretch of pushing, the bus springs into life and we set off. But not to worry, the time has been well-used as people chat and discuss and debate the day's events, and no one really seems to mind. After all, it is all quite normal...

Interesting by-products were a couple of insights the one pastor on our team had. Henry is from the far-western side of Uganda. He had never flown before and, during his sermon, shared how he had noticed that Kampala's greatest buildings, those which he had always seen as so big and impressive, looked like little toys. He shared that

God had spoken to him, chuckling at Henry's amazement, saying that He holds the whole earth in His palm and that what we see as big and impressive is actually quite small. He also shared on how, in his part of Uganda, women are mostly despised. He said that it was to such an extent that many men feel that a woman cannot hear from the Lord. He shared that meeting and seeing a woman pilot in action (loading and off-loading, flying around thunderstorms, etc.) had challenged these perceptions (many of which he personally did not condone) and he encouraged all men present to start listening to their wives and to start allowing them to have some input into the decisions been made.

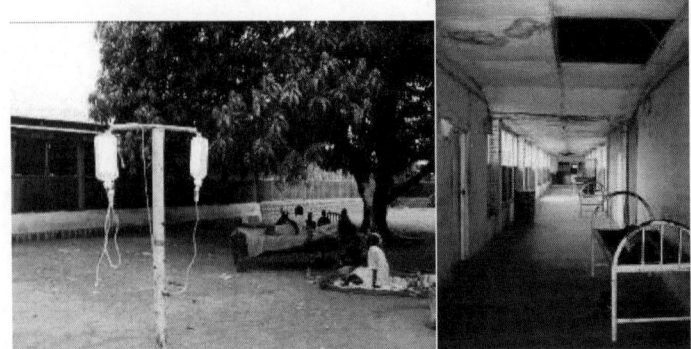

A trip last month to Aweil, near Darfur, with CBM, was also very interesting. Christian Blind Mission does a fantastic job; this trip was astounding in what it achieved. Hundreds of operations and hundreds more patients attended to for other eye-related illnesses. Eunice and Sture Nyholm really have an amazing heart for this ministry. Dr Sture was ill with something exotic but carried on regardless. Their whole team suffered from diarrhoea, so it was a rather tough 2 weeks for them. The reality is that, without MAF taking them there, this area would simply never have been visited. The flight up was long and the weather shocking. As I flew, a wall of black converged on my flight track. Had I been superstitious, I would have thought that it was surely the end of the world approaching! The cloud, as black as could be, extended up from the ground and stretched out as far as you could see. I tried to ascertain whether or not Rumbek, my refuelling stop, was clear of this or not; as I got closer I realised that it was somewhere within that beast and so I elected to fly to my alternative, Wau. The squall line pushed up vast amounts of sand ahead of it, dropping visibility to around 2 miles, and spent the rest of the day chasing me across Sudan as we both headed west. Wau was exceptionally Arabic, the menfolk being very curious but also very helpful. Old aircraft wrecks littered the edges of the runway and the unbearable heat rose up and mingled with the dust storm, together conspiring to produce a surreal setting in sickly yellow. I offloaded several hundred kilograms of medicine in Marial Bei and then proceeded to Aweil, where I would spend the night.

There was the obligatory long wait for the brigadier-in-charge, time spent with the rest of the soldiers playing dominoes beneath camouflage netting, and then the obligatory haggling over amounts to be paid for security and parking fees - you want to haggle hard but not so hard that they put you in gaol for the night! Ridiculous sums are demanded and whittled down to something reasonable, and comments like "You speak a lot for a woman!" are finally expelled in exasperation. Minutes later the heavens opened and we all ducked for cover. It would pour for the next 2 hours, leaving the runway totally unusable. Thank you Lord for letting me land first!!!

As you can see from the above pictures, the team was working in rather challenging circumstances. Darfur and the surrounding areas are not the best places to be. The hospital was part old colonial building (built by the British way back when) and part UN tents. The operations were carried out in a store-room; Members of the CBM team have to bring everything they need, down to a generator that runs the lamps and microscope that they use to see what they are doing! Eunice, a medical nurse and eye specialist, shared with me how many

people here suffer from River Blindness, to which there is no cure. Over the years folk have tried various things, the most effective being DDT, but that had its own disastrous side-effects. The best option would be to move out of these areas, but folk are adamant they will not leave their land. Besides, where would they go to?

Eunice told me how, in certain areas they have been to, around 70% of the villagers, of all ages, are partly or totally blind.

Their stuff was brought to the aircraft next day using the local transport. I made sure I didn't stand too close unless it bit…

❖   Praise God that we are all over our various rashes and flus.

❖   We thank Him for our continued safety on the roads and in the air.

❖   Our thanks for 2 nights away in the bush, where we tracked rhino on foot, were together as a family, and just rested and enjoyed His creation.

❖   Praise God for our maintenance and support staff, who work to keep our flights safe and our office ticking over as it should.

❖   Please pray as we prepare to go to court again this month; please uphold our lawyers and ask that God will give them wisdom and grant them and us favour before the Judge.

❖ We need to move house in mid-June; please pray that this will go well and not be too stressful. We will need to move again in late August if still here.

❖ And our prayer is that you would be blessed in every way; thank you so much for your love and support. You are the greatest blessing!

With our love and thanks,

Mike, D&I, and Laura.

Lord

Lord, standing on a mass grave is something just too terrible for words. I cannot begin to imagine what people here have been through. All I know is that You are the only real answer to this. Thank You for the ministry of Sam and Sarah Tsapwe and for the friendship we enjoy. Thank You that MAF gets to fly them to places like this and that we get to share The Good News of You and Your plan. Thank You for Your Church in this place, a corner of light in the darkness and an island of hope within a sea of despair.

I pray for those in Aweil; what a challenging place to be! Please send many here who will help to rebuild this abandoned part of Sudan; it needs so much. Please grow Your church here and protect the Christians who are quite liable to suffer persecution.

Nothing could prepare me for the "NO" the Judge handed down with respect to our adoption request. I have never felt angrier or more distraught before, never. I was so expecting it to be "YES". It made my wheels fall off, as they say. Life turned itself upside down and, once the cauldron of emotions was under control, the work really began again in earnest. Yet if I compare that to Darfur, to what I have seen in Aweil, it is nothing. You have blessed me with choices and the ability to do and be; most here do not have that luxury. Our path may seem rocky but here people live in 'rocky day after day.' I know You are with me; my prayer is that they, too, will come to know and understand You are with them.

Amen.

News from Mike and Laura: August 2009

Dearest Friends and Family

I seem to have spent most of the last few months catching up with old friends all over the place! It has been a real time of blessing! I got to 'do tea' with a Linda, a missionary friend in Torrit, Sudan, of African Inland Mission. I brought the biscuits and she provided the tea and lots of interesting information about the work of AIM. One of its teams has just had to be evacuated from Sudan; the team members were accused of stealing the rain and literally had to flee for their lives. All over the globe AIM folk are busy translating the Bible into local languages (to name one of their ministries), living amongst the local people as they do, normally in challenging conditions - this time in very dangerous conditions! But it served to highlight the seriousness of the drought that has taken hold of Sudan and northern Uganda this year. Many folk will starve, many are already. Please do pray for rain.

WHM (World Harvest Mission) has a medical mission in the far western part of Uganda, along the Congolese border. It was to this mission that I transported an 'MK' (missionary kid) who was coming home from boarding-school in Kenya. This young lad had grown into something of a skyscraper since I saw him last and one almost needed a shoe-horn to get him into the little C206 along with his school boxes, etc. I called his mum prior to departing Entebbe to say he was on his way (mums need to know these things!!!) and their whole team of around 20 folk, together with around 20 villagers, came out to meet him, so he had quite the reception party! It was great seeing his mum's overjoyed face, share the happiest of family reunions, and catch up on the news with them all. That's one of the great things about my job: getting to know so many interesting people, learning about what God is doing through them, sharing, in a small part, some of their joys and sadnesses and simply making it possible for a kid to go home to mum safely.

World Harvest Mission also has a team in Mundri, Sudan. I was fortunate enough to take a group there which was going to be teaching at the Bible College. One of the gentlemen, Joshua, is Sudanese and it was a special trip for him. You see, it would be the first time he had been home to Sudan since fleeing the war as a young boy. He was going to meet his mother, the first time he had seen her in over a decade. He was so excited, close to tears for most of the 2-hour flight, constantly tapping me on the shoulder and asking: "Where are we now? Ah, yes, that is my uncle's village, this is where we hid, and this is the river to…" I was even more thrilled to be able to pick the team up 10 says later and find out that though there had been challenges, as he had to wrestle with where he now 'fits in' and the sadness of departing again, his reunion with his mother had been better than he had ever hoped it would be. I couldn't help but wonder how many times this devout Christian man has prayed that God would make a way for him to go home and of how God had enabled that, partly through MAF, partly though you.

Now the C206 is small, taking a maximum of 6 people. Having said that, the longer the flight, the more fuel you have to carry, the less weight (people and freight) you can carry. (Long flight, lots of Bibles, so only one passenger.) On a 7-hour flight it can also seem VERY slow so, on such occasions, it is always a real blessing to have a chatty passenger with an interesting story to tell! Somewhere up near the southern Darfur border someone had scraped away the edges of the road, flattened it a bit and declared it to be a runway. And so aerial access to Lunyaker, an almost invisible village without even a dot on a map to herald its existence, was born. The H.A.R.T. foundation, headed by Baroness Cox, is one of MAF's partners, and it is funding a project up here. So it was that I met Eunice, a teacher from the UK. We had flown another lady, plus a full load of teaching materials, up the week before. Now Eunice was to join her. The two ladies were working firstly to teach the children (under a tree at this stage) and secondly to assess how they can train the local teachers, as most of them only have around 3-4 years of education themselves. They will return next year to train the teachers.

A week later we picked Eunice up (she was swimming the English Channel in a few weeks to raise funds for a charity!!!) and she came to dinner, which was a real treat for Deborah and Ivan and something of an ear-bashing for Eunice! The interesting thing is that there really is no other way for Eunice to get to Lunyaker other than with MAF; no one goes there. I just marvel at how God's plans for those children and those Sudanese teachers are being worked out though groups like the H.A.R.T. Foundation and volunteers like Eunice spending their holidays in such invisible places doing such invisible things.

One of my favourite stops in Sudan is Nimule, where Far Reaching Ministries (FRM) has a mission. Over the years I have become good friends with Vicky, the lady who leads the team there. On one flight home from Juba to Entebbe, the weather was so appalling I could not get through. Happily I was close to Nimule so landed there. I got to spend a splendid morning chatting to Vicky and several other ladies over coffee! The ladies were all making preparations for the annual graduation of Chaplains to the Sudanese army! FRM trains soldiers in its Bible school for 12 months and then they return into the army as chaplains, so spreading the Gospel as well as providing pastoral care to the soldiers of the Sudanese army. It was a morning of fellowship with sisters! A few days later I flew back again, this time taking in Wes, Vicky's husband, as well as 12 other team members who would help teach at a Bible conference. All the previously-graduated chaplains come for a week-long annual refresher course; they travel from all over Sudan, many taking a week or so to reach Nimule. All the chaplains were on parade to meet us. You get to know one or two a bit better than the rest, and it is always interesting to hear about where they are now and what they are doing, who has got married, that they have a child now... And it always brings a smile to see these soldiers with the cross on their lapels and to know that so many Sudanese will hear the Good News through them.

And then, quite suddenly, life turned through 90 degrees!

I can scarcely believe that I am sitting here in Kent writing this email to you all! In our last newsletter, June 2009, we asked you all to pray for the paperwork needed for Deborah's and Ivan's UK citizenship to be processed. We were told to expect late September and then a few weeks to process their passports. Well, a lot of folk must have been praying pretty hard, because on Tuesday we received a call from the High Commission advising us that their UK citizenship was approved and to please come in tomorrow with the passport applications. We took these in on Wednesday, and on Friday we had their passports!!! With the owners of the house we were living in due to arrive in a few weeks time, our Land Rover limping its way to the scrap-yard and the replacement pilot and family arriving in late August, it was amazing and very much welcomed news!

Before I knew it I was saying goodbye to Liila in the Congo, a wonderful chap who works as an operations officer in Bunia and, amongst other things, translates from French to English for me when I have to deal with the officials there. Then it was the last flight in Uganda (I managed to fly Deborah and Ivan from Kajjansi to Entebbe - just after sunrise - poor Mike!!!),and then the last flight to Sudan. A flurry of box and suitcase packing followed and, before we knew it, it was the farewell party. It was so hard to say goodbye to friends and colleagues! We had come to learn and to serve and we have been so blessed in the process! We leave Uganda the proud parents of 2 lovely children (well, most of the time, anyhow!), a wealth of flying 'on wings to serve' and the privilege of meeting many wonderful people along the way. At our farewell Steve (our programme manager) told us that Mike had flown the equivalent of 2 times around the earth, and I, 7 times. In the thousands of miles we flew neither of us ever had an emergency, an incident, or even scratched the aircraft. Of the hundreds of miles driven along treacherous roads, we never had even one vehicle accident - not even a bump! We never caught malaria or suffered any serious injury or illness. At times we felt ready to break, but we never did. At times we felt we could give up, but we were sustained. At times we cried, but our joy always returned. And we want to thank you as we TRULY KNOW and TRULY BELIEVE that God has honoured the hundreds, if not thousands, of prayers which have been offered up by YOU for us. We know that without you this would have been impossible and we want to thank you from the bottom of our hearts for your love and support. We pray that God blesses each one of you right out of your socks!!! We thank and praise God for keeping us safe, healthy and encouraged. And we thank and praise Him for you.

In our last newsletter I wrote:

We still are not sure what the next few months hold for us and still do not know 'where next' and 'when'. We know that God is in control and that He has a plan for us as a family, but it is still difficult waiting at times. Please do pray for us as we seek His way and His will.

This remains true!! We are now in the UK on an extended furlough as we finalize the children's citizenship. We will be working with MAF UK to promote the new Kodiak aircraft (this is just SOOO exciting!) during October and November, something we are both very much looking forward to. With regards to Mongolia, due to a wide range of reasons, there is some uncertainty as to whether or not MAF needs another pilot at this stage. So, we are not quite sure where we will be heading next! But, on my last flight, I had a huge thunderstorm system go past and afterwards a rainbow! God's reminder to us that He has a plan. So, please, do keep praying for us and especially for Deborah and Ivan as they adjust to living in the UK for the next few months.

With our love and thanks for all you have made possible
and for those you have helped to reach,

Mike, Deborah, Ivan and Laura.

"He will cover you with His feathers, and under his
wings you will find refuge." Psalm 91:4.

*Lord, I know that our time here is coming to an end. I find
myself filled with many mixed emotions. You have taught us so
much, You have changed me, You have grown me. I'd very much
like to know what is next but I know You are just asking us to
trust You and to wait, so there it is.*

Thank You for the many wonderful friends I have made here; for the many missionaries I have met, for the many people You have crossed my path with. I have seen change for the better here and I know that MAF has had a large part to play in that; I praise You for that and I thank You for MAF.

I have seen You in people I have met, I have seen You in things they have done, I have seen You answer prayers and care for many.

You have shown me more of how Your body works. I have come to value in a profoundly deep way those who stay and pray; I thank You for them because I know that they are an integral part of Your plan. Their faithfulness makes for MAF's success, our safety and Your glory.

Lord, we came as 2, we leave as a family of 4. Thank You for Mike and Deborah and Ivan; they are my greatest blessing.

Amen.

News from Mike and Laura: June 2009

It probably will never change: that quiet thrill one experiences as the Land Rover bumps and rattles around the corner and I turn onto the road that leads to Kajjansi airfield. There, as always, Lake Victoria, regal and majestic and very well-named, slides into view. I am normally just in time, as today, to see the sun slice its way through the horizon as it starts the day's journey west. The air is blissfully cool, webs glimmer with dew and a thin white line of low cloud hangs precariously over the marshland adjacent to the runway. 'Critters' (an unusual word I have learnt from our cousins across the Pond; describes all manner of little animals) and bugs scurry about, long-horned cows start the day's munching and passengers start arriving. Soon the cool will give way to heat and dust and sweat but, for now, loading and unloading will be sweat-free. Well, almost...

My aircraft sits gleaming, cleaned by the faithful aircraft handlers late yesterday afternoon. As I pre-flight her, running my hands and eyes over rivets and bolts, scrutinising engine and propeller, fuel and oil and all manner of things, I am thankful for the engineers who so faithfully maintain her. Recently, a friend flying for another organization had his engine stop just after take-off. No one was injured but the aircraft was seriously damaged. As ever, I am grateful for the sharp eyes and a professional calling our engineers have. The sky is almost clear, save for a few high clouds striking across the sky, so betraying the strong headwind I will encounter once airborne. A few fluffy little ones here and there, the promise of thunderstorms and turbulence later on. Best check on the SicSacs…

I fly 2 hours from A to B, picking up Christian Blind Mission. They have just done 2 weeks' worth of sight-saving eye operations. They are all dusty and weary, but very fulfilled. We fly B to C. As I help the passenger enter the rear of the aircraft, he asks: "What about the security situation at E? Your aircraft has been threatened with ambush!" Eleven sets of very wide eyes snap around and meet mine! I ask them all to wait and I dash off towards the pit-latrines, where I know I will find a signal for the cell phone, and call a friend at E. Yes, he tells me, my info is correct and he is talking with MAF Ops in Kampala. We agree on signals and a plan of action. I call the office and a safety plan is set in motion. We fly C to D, where I off-load all of the passengers bar the one going to E; I will pick them all up later. We wait at D until the military are in place and all precautions have been taken, not only by us but by those who will travel by road to E. We arrive at E, one 'special' approach later and we land. Six minutes later we are on our way again, one off, one on. We are all safe; I am mindful of God's provision and His hand upon us all. So many options for 'what if we never knew'. We pick up those at D and head home. It is Monday.

Tuesday. We all get up very early, having packed everything we might need the night before, and dress up for the occasion. D&I, Mike and I all pile into our Landie and head off into the traffic. We stop-start our way to the High Court, meet our lawyer and discover that we have left the file with all the originals behind!! One of those "But I thought you brought the flag" moments; at the top of Everest and neither of us had remembered to replace the file in the bag, having added one last paper the night before. I am not sure whether to cry or laugh. A young lad appears; he is on workexperience and will be sitting in on our hearing. Hmmm. We are summoned and enter Court. The Judge peers up at us over her spectacles. We all sit on invitation and remain deathly quiet. Our lawyer presents her case. The youth, sitting alongside me, leans his head back on his chair and closes his eyes for a nap.

My heart stops. Call it maternal instinct or whatever you like, but I jab onesaid youth in the ribs and hiss at him, hoping that his life is flashing before his eyes! Hopefully the Judge has not noticed. D&I give us 30 minutes of perfect stillness and quiet and then those little muscles and mouths can remain still no longer. Our lawyer presents the case and, around 2 hours later, we are dismissed. We are asked to return on Thursday for the ruling. I ask to be excused as I will be flying and there is no way I will be able to change that at such late notice. The Judge agrees; Mike will go alone.

Wednesday. I flew around Uganda, supervising another pilot through his annual route check. All went well… Loads of NGOs safely sent all over Uganda.

Thursday. D-Day! I am flying all over Southern Sudan today; Mike will fight the traffic. Later I will learn that he spent 4 hours waiting his turn, only to discover that 'our' documents had been left behind by the Court. Being the patient soul he is, he persevered and the ruling was given. We had agreed that Mike would not say anything until I got home, so that I wasn't distracted whilst flying. So, having just landed at Maridi and switched on my phone, I was surprised to see an sms from Mike come through. He hadn't been able to contain his joy; the Judge had granted us adoption! Well, I was so thrilled I think that I flew home without the engine! Revd Patricia, flying out from Maridi to Entebbe, was on hand to share both my joy and the silly grin on my face. Finally, the hardest bit was over. It was great getting home to Mike and the kids that night. Finally, 100% legally a family!

Friday. I had never heard of Watoto until I arrived here in Uganda. It is a wonderful family thing. A large church here set up a 'village' where hundreds of orphans could live in small groups of 8 with house-parents in their own home. It's for life. These children are blessed with a life-long family. Each year children from the Watoto village travel the world as a choir, singing (See www.watoto.com). This trip (each child normally only goes once) helps to broaden the child's experience as well as educate the audience, whilst raising funds to run the village. There is a high number of orphans in Uganda due to both the recently-ended civil war waged by the LRA and HIV/AIDS. The team leading recognised that there was a need to help young women, who had escaped from the LRA, to rebuild their lives. From this, Living Hope was born. At present around 1000 women are in training in Kampala. The ladies receive tailoring or business skills training as well as Bible-based discipleship. Many give their hearts to the Lord. In August 2008 these 2 projects, Watoto and Living Hope, expanded into Gulu, Northern Uganda.

Gulu: famous as a town that housed night–commuters during the civil war. Children would walk from their villages each night to sleep in shelters or the street. The alternative was being abducted by the LRA, mutilated, murdered, raped and forced to carry a gun and use it as directed. So it was with much enthusiasm that I flew Marilyn and her team of 4 up to Gulu for the day. Living Hope, Gulu, has 50 ladies learning tailoring. 40 ladies have recently completed business skills training. Food is distributed once a month to HIV+ ladies so that they are well enough to continue taking their ARV medication which prolongs life, so enabling them to care for their own children and to lead a normal life. It is quite a large compound. The amazing thing is that it shows God has heard their cries! The entire compound used to be night shelters! The local government has now donated these shelters to the church and it has been turned into a training centre. A nursery school is complete, awaiting only toys and furnishings. A dining area is nearing completion, as is a coffee house where folk will be able to buy ground coffee. A Babies' Home is planned for late 2010, as well as a hospital in the near future. It's all about getting ladies, who no one wants, off 'hand-outs' and equipping them to be self-reliant as well as teaching them about the Lord. All of the ladies are offered counselling as they have all been through the most horrific experiences. Years of living in the bush as 'wives' to LRA soldiers have left them without any form of education and with HIV+.

I was shown around the compound by a young lady, Gladys, 24. She had seen her father murdered by the LRA. An uncle had taken her in, put her through school and she had trained as a teacher. Now here she was, teaching others and praising God for the great work in her life. Quite a lady!!

Marilyn, who travels the world speaking about these projects, educating and fund-raising, had spoken in New Zealand. A pastor there, Maree, had heard her and wanted to come and share with these ladies. The morning was a Ladies' Service, at which both Maree and Marilyn spoke. The singing, all in Acholi, was just fantastic and a joyful outpouring of praise. The ladies danced and danced as brightly-coloured, tattered rags became the garments of salvation and royal robes of righteousness that Isaiah writes of before my very eyes. Despised and rejected 'former abductees' became daughters of the Living King. Maree, whose childhood and youth had involved the loss of both parents, and abuse and rape, was able to share about God's transforming power in her own life. She'd been where they'd been and so spoke with the authority of experience.

I met Nancy, shy and quiet, who didn't really want to look you in the eye. She smiled and hugged Marilyn; Nancy has a new nose. Someone had sponsored a plastic surgery operation that gave her a new nose. Someone else had discipled her and led her to the Lord. Nancy is still praying for new lips and new ears, because they too were hacked off, but there is now an inner healing that has commenced and Nancy is slowly healing from the inside out.

I met Santa, tall and thin, fighting HIV. She's learnt how to sew and is now earning a living, able to buy food and pay for her children to go to school. Her dignity has been restored. She too, has found Jesus and was healing from the inside out.

We flew back late that day, just as the thunderstorms were all dying out and the sun heading off to bed. At times one can be frustrated by not being able to really get in there and help in a more hands-on sort of way. But, well, someone has to be the donkey. And that's MAF; the donkey in the parable of the Good Samaritan. We often never know what difference those we fly make, but I do know that each flight that you make possible makes a difference, the difference.

And yesterday, flying around in Uganda, I had to spend 2 hours at Matany. Security in the Kaabong area meant I could not land there and would have to wait for the soldiers to secure the area. It was a gift! Father Marco of the Comboni Brothers invited me for coffee…

Father Marco is around 75. He started working in this inhospitable part of Uganda at the age of 27. He is quiet and grey, his eyes twinkle and his hands betray the years of hard labour he has given under the harsh African sun. I asked him how he had managed 50+ years out here. He just smiled and said: "Oh, my child, it feels like it has only been a moment." The men and women serving there were so kind and gentle and loving to each other. They treated the Ugandans around them with such love and respect, spoke all their languages so fluently, stopped to help someone with a burden, greeted, with time and patience, each one who came by as if they were the most important person that they would meet that day. The little lounge, very simple and clean, betrayed their hearts: little birthday lists, prayer lists for friends and family, theology books and books on prayer and service, and mission magazines. I just felt the presence of Christ; the peace, the love, the servant heart. This truly was an oasis in a desert. God just loved me that day through them; I feel so privileged, so challenged. I felt like a donkey that had been given a huge bunch of fresh carrots…

On the family front, we moved house last weekend! So it was "All change, please, all change", and a great opportunity for a clear out! Thank you for your prayers, as it was not easy. Mike's muscles got a good work-out, as did the Landie. He was quite the hero and very long-suffering in doing most of the moving of stuff whilst I packed and cleaned. D&I were quite 'disrupted' by it all and spent most of the day helping or getting into or out of trouble! They finished school on Thursday and so are now on a 2-month summer holiday, so please do pray for Mike. It is great to have them home but always a challenge to keep 2 such busy little things occupied and out of mischief. Kitty stayed in our old home and has been taken on by the new owners. Or is that the other way around?! We now have a dog, Chewy, who 'comes' with this house. D&I are slowly getting used to her; she is bouncy and big and has very large, white teeth!!! In 2 months we will need to move again, so please do keep on praying for our paperwork for British citizenship for D&I to come through.

We still are not sure what the next few months hold for us and still do not know 'where next' and 'when'. We know that God is in control and that He has a plan for us as a family, but it is still difficult waiting at times. Please do pray for us as we seek His way and His will.

Thank you for your love, your support and your partnership with us in this amazing journey. God bless you. With our love and thanks,

Mike, D&I and Laura. Oh, and Chewy.

"Give thanks to the Lord for He is good." Psalm 136:1.

Lord, thank You for father Marco and the encouragement he was to me today! Thank You that You send little reminders of Your care and Your nearness.

Thank You for Mike and his servant heart, for his unwavering support, for his dedication to our family, for his ability to be true to himself regardless of what others may feel he should be doing or being.

Thank You for D&I, for all the joy and challenge they bring. For their laughter that warms the heart and for the way they show me more of what You are like.

Thank You for people who have big vision, who make great things happen and impact on thousands. Thank You for those who are willing to have a small part and simply pray faithfully day after day. Thank You for those who are moved to do whatever You call them to do.

Amen.

Held aloft on prayer:
7 October 2009

We left knowing we would learn more than teach, receive more than give, and grow within ourselves. They have to have been four of the most interesting years of my life! We 'wrote home' to our friends and supporters quite simply because we knew that they loved us and held us aloft in prayer, and because we loved them for their care and their faithfulness.

There is only so much you can write in newsletters. They show only a part of our lives with MAF. A thousand things happened about which we have never written. Over the years Mike and I just knew that 'that' amazing encounter with so-and-so, or the close shave with a demented taxi-driver, or the snakes that never got near us, were all God honouring the prayers of our faithful supporters. We are forever meeting people in Church who have supported MAF for 1, 2, 20, 30, or 40 years! MAF has been successfully operating since just after World War II; what a witness to their faithfulness!

If you are thinking of going out to the mission field, whether in your street, town, or on another continent, may we encourage you to treasure your supporters? Their love is something quite special; unique, uplifting and empowering.

If you support someone on the mission field, thank you! Please know that it is impossible to work on the mission field without your prayers and support. We knew we were prayed for and that gave us great strength through our dark times, and it helped us to keep focused during all the other times. Know, too, that God values highly your prayers and that what you offer up is a fragrant sacrifice to the Lord.

With our love,

Mike and Laura.

News from Mike and Laura
12 October 2009

If you are 'into' aircraft, Duxford is a special place. Arriving just after 8am, our team was met by a faint orange smudge struggling through the low grey clouds, the black tarmac shining with the rain, and the quiet shuffle of flight-line officials getting ready. Large 1940's hangars, the original WW2 buildings, and a few Rapides poking their noses at you set you back 60 years! You walk past aviation history, watching the shapes and curves of aircraft change, the size and type of engine evolve; each one painted to reflect her own particular character, her own particular role. You walk past row upon row of aircraft that have been used to win wars and, at great cost, our peace here in the UK, as well as many used to transport passengers around the globe.

But nestled between two WW2 hangars, and alongside the Duxford Spitfire, 2009 catches up with you in a special way. For there, MAF's new Kodiak aircraft sat twinkling: red, white and blue. Here sat an aircraft designed specifically to bring hope, relief and purpose to thousands of lives. She is rugged and petite, sturdy and beautiful. She has been made by hands that believe in the best that God has to offer, is *en route* to Kalimantan, (a remote island where people are simply cut off from everything) and will be flown, maintained and organized by a team of people who are dedicated to seeing God's hope and life brought to thousands. Like those who supported MAF, she is unassuming and will serve for years in quiet obscurity.

The MAF trailer was there, together with a large group of MAF volunteers. We spoke to many people, handed out a lot of information, and showed many folk around the

Kodiak. There was a constant stream of people to speak to! Mike spoke to many about the aircraft and Deborah and Ivan helped to hand out leaflets. They were very good! ☺

It was amazing to have Stuart King, who founded MAF in 1945, head-up our team. After completing much time in Europe, he was later based at Duxford during WW2, where he served as Chief Technical Officer. Being back on this particular airfield and at this particular air show event was particularly significant to Stuart. The Duxford Air Show organizers had asked to interview Stuart and myself. We thank God for this amazing opportunity to share about the work God is doing through MAF to a large group of people who would otherwise never hear about MAF or think about God using aeroplanes.

It was also very special to be a part of a team, each one united and working towards a common goal. Thank you all for the prayers you gave that contributed towards the wonderful success of this event. Please do continue to pray for Harry, Derek, Bryan and myself, and the large team of organizers as we fly the Kodiak to various locations in the UK. Pray for favour, safety, good weather and good health. And join us as we praise and thank God for this wonderful new aircraft and for all those who will be blessed though it.

Much love, God bless, Mike, D&I and Laura.

Dear Friends and Family

WOW! Thank you all for praying! We very much felt you were with us and we are so thankful to you all!

It was quite a day. We had to leave the house by 0715hrs to be at the court at 0830hrs, due to the traffic. (It's only about 20km away!) That was where the first prayer was answered, as we arrived on time and the traffic was way lighter than usual. Amazing!

We even had time to have a cup of tea in the canteen.

The second major answer to prayer was that the Judge did indeed arrive. We were told it was unlikely he would make it due to other commitments, but to come regardless.

We had quite a long wait but we had packet books, crayons, etc. to keep the children occupied, so they spent the time colouring whilst we all stood in the corridor. No talking allowed!

Another answer to prayer was our maintaining our patience (we prayed specifically in this area as it can be quite frustrating not being told when or how it all works, being totally at the mercy of others, working within a foreign system, etc.) and another was the children being calm and quiet for two-and-a-half hours!

The Judge was very demanding (as all Judges should be). He asked some questions which our lawyer was unable to explain clearly, so I was given the microphone (it all gets tape-recorded) and answered his questions as clearly as I could.

He was not happy with the Care Order. This document we were not even aware of until 5 months ago, at which point we (along with a whole bunch of other families) rushed out and obtained the order. He feels the 3 years should start from that date. This means we will need to foster them for another 2 years and 7 months. At this point in the discussion Mike and I started playing with the kids, as we were both quite alarmed at it and felt it best to just leave it in His hands!

So, we have a lot of praises to offer. Please do, however, continue to pray for us; that the ruling on the 25th will be positive and without additional complications. Mike and I have attempted to meet each legal requirement as best we can, in all good faith with the information we have available and to honour God in how we have done it.

The Judge has told us that he will give his ruling next Wednesday, the 25th.

We had a party at 5pm (faith in action!), and a huge and special thank you to all those MAF kiddies who came and celebrated Deborah's and Ivan's Adoption Day. We will all be sleeping very soundly tonight.

With much love and sincere thanks,

Mike, D&I and Laura.

Lord, what a day! How we need You! How do folk survive without You? At times today I just wanted to cry out of sheer frustration; how did we manage to find the worst traffic jam of the year?! But You got us there on time! It doesn't sound as if it went that well today; help us to keep on trusting You. Thank You that we have each other and that we have You. I pray for those who are less fortunate than us, who go through this without the knowledge of You in their lives. I pray for the many children here who remain in orphanages and who never make it into a family of their own. Lord, please be their dad and reveal Yourself to them in a deep and powerful way. Amen.

News from Mike and Laura: November 2009

Dear Friends and Family

Today I found myself sitting in a chair listening to two MAF founders, Stuart King and Jack Cummins, speak of the 'early days'; days spent getting MAF 'off the ground', as it were. We were sitting in the lounge at Lydd airport, them both having just flown in the Kodiak. As they relayed story upon story, you could just see that their passion now is a strong as it has ever been. I felt as if I were on hallowed ground! What an amazing privilege it was to just meet them both and to listen to them share about MAF. So amazing to think that, all these years later, that which they so faithfully started has grown under God's care into the far-reaching entity MAF is now!

Our family has been in the UK for 3 months now and it has been quite special. Who would have ever guessed that we would have been asked to help with the 'Kodiak Tour'? We guess it's: "For such a time as this!" And it has been wonderful! It has been an immense pleasure and joy to fly an MAF aircraft around the UK and meet so many of our supporters! People have come out in their hundreds to see the aircraft, rain or shine. Well, mostly rain, actually! This particular Kodiak will soon be on its way to Kalimantan in Indonesia, where it will bring relief and hope to people in that troubled part of the world. Yet we have flown it the length and breadth of our beautiful British Isles, thinking of you and praying for you as we have quietly zoomed over your heads.

We have visited White Waltham, Exeter, Sywell, Biggin Hill, Lydd, the Isle of Man and Carlisle. In Carlisle we got to see first-hand the response to the terrible flooding up there, and our hearts and prayers go out to all of you dealing with that at the moment. To see the highly-trained Sea King helicopter rescue crews, along with the mountain rescue and Police, spring into action just really highlighted the difference between here and the many places in which we serve. In many of the countries where MAF operates, there are simply not the resources for such a sophisticated and well-resourced response.

In the Isle of Man we met the wonderful people who have funded this aircraft. At Sywell we met a fantastic group of teenagers who are now all signed up to 'Above and Beyond', the new MAF youth 'wing'; look out for great things from these young adults! I had many people who are either learning to fly or are already pilots speak to me about how they should go about preparing for MAF or how to apply. We managed to get many youngsters to 'sit up front' in the cockpit, and I'm sure we've encouraged a few to think about being pilots when they grow up! For many people who have supported MAF for all their adult lives, the opportunity to not only see close up, but to actually sit in, an MAF aircraft was an exceedingly special one.

The Dutch pilot, Harry Berghuis, has flown for MAF in Indonesia and PNG for 15 years and I learnt a lot from him, not only about flying but about MAF's work in that area and about him and his family, too. It was also a great opportunity to get to know many people working in the MAF offices in Folkestone, as they got to experience flying with MAF themselves along with getting to know us all better. We've had a lot of laughs!

This Saturday will be our last Kodiak 'event'; we will hold a MAF Supporter Open Day, and I'm sure we will see many more of you there. Bring your wellies; it's wet! And then we will have to say goodbye to this lovely Kodiak and leave her to get on with her trip to Kalimantan.

On the family side of things, at this point, our useful contribution to the work of MAF here in the UK will be over. We still have a few months to go in the UK as we finalise the children's citizenship. Mike and I have prayed about it and we have decided that I will work 'outside' of MAF for the next 3½ months, so that any support you send will be used when we go back to the field around April/May 2010. We recognise that times are tough here in the UK and very much want to use your support wisely. So please do continue to support us and please, please, do keep praying for us!

Approximately 4 weeks ago MAF HQ advised us that we will no longer be going to Mongolia, as things there have changed and they no longer need us there. We have been asked to go back to Africa, as we are now needed there, so that is where we will be heading off to.

With all the travelling about it has been a real blessing to have 'daddy' doing the teaching; Mike is a natural teacher and both Deborah and Ivan really enjoy the home schooling. So many thanks to all of you who have prayed for those issues; God has been faithful and it is all working out even better than we had expected. Both children are experiencing their first autumn ("Mmummy, where have all the leaves gone...?") as well as their first winter ("Daddy, where has the sun gone...why is it dark so much...?"), and have both settled in exceedingly well. They are now 'Beavers', a part of the Scouting movement, as well as very lively members of their new Sunday-School! Mike and I will celebrate our sixth wedding anniversary on 29 November and I still think he is fantastic and absolutely adorable; thanks to all of you who regularly pray for our family and our marriage.

I am due to go in for a small 'op' (girlie plumbing) on 3 December. I have, in my mitts, a letter stating that I am not allowed to use any machinery for 3 whole days, including an oven or washing machine! Yep, it's there in black and white!!! So, Mike will be cooking for a bit! Pizza, day 1, McDonald's day 2 and something from the 'ready-made' aisle at Tesco on day 3… Seriously though, please do pray for the both of us; Mike with his hands full and me as I recover.

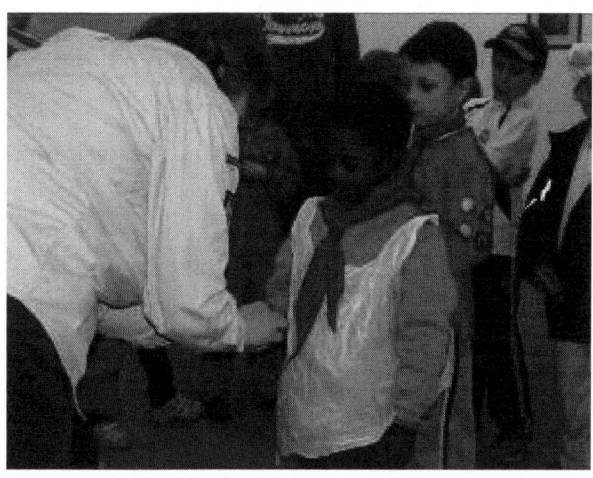

We will continue to visit as many churches over the next 3½ months as possible, and look forward to meeting as many of you as we can. I will do my best to send out emails with details of where and when as we go along. We praise and thank God for providing us with work for the next few months and ask that you hold us in prayer as I do so; I will be working as an air traffic controller at Shoreham Airport and we would value your prayers as we up sticks and change location again.

We would also like to wish each one of you a very blessed and a very happy Christmas. We pray that you get time to be with your families and loved ones and we pray that God bless each one of you throughout 2010.

Thank you so much for the support and prayers you give to both MAF and to our family.

With all our love and thanks,

Mike, Deborah, Ivan and Laura.

Flying In Faith - A message from us to you: September 2011

You see, it's not about the aircraft, it's about the people. The aircraft is just a means to an end. I had the great privilege in November 2009 of sitting and listening to Jack Hemmings and Stuart King as they talked about how they got MAF 'off the ground'. They had people and the needs of the people in the developing world on their hearts. What they thought would work out to be around, say, 12 aircraft serving missionaries and aid workers in Africa, has blossomed into something quite breathtaking; over 150 aircraft serving in over 35 countries from over 65 bases into over 2,900 airstrips. And this is a story in its own right; how Godly men and women ran with their God-given dream, discarding all those who said it couldn't be done or shouldn't be done, trusting God at His word and His promises, and founded MAF. And my, how God has faithfully nurtured and grown MAF throughout the decades!

It's a story about the hundreds of thousands of people whose lives have been touched through the quiet 'background' work of MAF.

I meet these sorts of people on each and every flight.

Like Sarah, a young lady whose lips, nose and ears have been hacked off by the Lord's Resistance Army in Uganda, who has been forced to murder her own family and then abducted and forced to be a 'wife' to an LRA commander, being left HIV-positive before managing to escape. It's about the folk in the back of my MAF aircraft that I have flown in who will be taking her to have reconstructive surgery, providing trauma counselling along with reconciliation training to her and hundreds of others for many years to come.

About a little boy, Matthew, violently convulsing and slowly dying of meningitis; the 18-hour drive to Kampala over rough tracks and through the bush would kill him. It's about a distraught mother clinging to his quivering body as I land, bursting into tears at the sight of the aircraft and the doctor that climbs out the back of it to treat her son. About a life-saving flight of just 1 hour that transports mother and child to Kampala, where they are whisked off to a hospital where he makes a full recovery.

MAF is about people like Bishop Anthony Pogo of Kajo Keji in Sudan, who is working tirelessly to help rebuild the lives of those in his diocese; lives wrecked by decades of war, blighted by the lack of infrastructure and by poverty and overwhelming needs. Our flights help to rebuild Sudan as we fly in hundreds of skilled aid- and church-workers who help him, and many others like him, work towards a better future, so touching life upon life.

Our faith drives us; God lights a fire in each of our hearts, a passion not just for flying but for people and for seeing His love, His hope and His promises fulfilled in the lives of people all over the globe.

The poverty, the pain and the hopelessness of a refugee camp are hard to describe. Haggard, war-wearied men, emaciated women and screaming babies with distended stomachs are there to greet many a landing. Yet, amidst the sea of suffering we often walk into, we see His gracious love at work in those we fly. We know that behind us, each seat in our aircraft is filled with a passenger who is the answer to the prayer someone suffering has lifted before His throne of grace. MAF is about our family, about us growing as we learn through those God places around us to shape us and mould us as we work though our ugly bits.

MAF is also about people like you, who believe in what God is doing though MAF. You may never meet a single person MAF has flown, or ever get to see first-hand the difference your support makes. Yet through God's immense goodness your prayers and your support keep us airborne and make it possible for us to be where we are doing what we are doing: Flying for Life.

We never did make it to Mongolia. Once back in the UK finalizing the UK side of Deborah's and Ivan's adoption, we were asked by MAF to go to Kenya instead. It was a time of great uncertainty and, once again, it was knowing that so many were standing with us in prayer that helped us through the range of emotions; a deep sadness at not going to Mongolia, the excitement and uncertainty of going to Kenya, and the pleasure and exhaustion of driving hundreds of miles around the UK fund-raising with two home-schooled children in tow!

Kenya itself was as unique a posting as Uganda had been. We saw and experienced so many amazing things and saw God's hand at work in so many ways. By Easter 2011 we knew that God was asking us to move on. Had we heard right?! A thousand questions bombarded us as a couple, and we sought the counsel of some of our most dear supporters as they agreed to intercede in prayer for us. The answer came and, once again, our children were asked to move life and school as we moved back to the UK. The last half of 2011 was a time of great adjustment. Our supporters were amazing and loved us and prayed for us as we struggled to find our feet; it was especially difficult for Deborah and Ivan, and it was six months before we managed to get them into the same school. As 2011 drew to a close and we wrote our last newsletter, we suffered a profound sense of loss as we had to say "goodbye" to our MAF 'family' of supporters. Yet we gained a deep sense of appreciation for the magnitude and importance of God's greater family and believe that God is using our experiences to enable us to take our turn supporting mission in the UK and abroad. Thank you and God bless you.

With love, Mike Bundy and Laura Westley, together with Deborah and Ivan.

"Now may our God and Father Himself and our Lord Jesus clear the way for us to come to you." 1 Thessalonians 3 v 11.

"For over 60 years, pilots have enabled MAF's ministry to reach out to thousands of needy people across the developing world. But it takes a team of people to keep pilots and planes in the air, overcoming barriers to bring the Gospel in word and action to people who need it so desperately.

Without supporters like you, none of this would be possible. We want you on our team too. If you would like to know more, please get in touch with us."

Meyers, M. 2000, 'Eyes Turned Skyward', Kent, MAF.

UK: www.maf-uk.org

USA: www.maf.org

South Africa: www.mafsa.co.za

More books on MAF include ' Hope has Wings' by Stuart King, 'Many Adventures Followed' by Roger Young, 'Jungle Pilot' by Russell. T. Hitt, 'Eyes Turned Skywards' by Max Meyers and 'Betty Green – Wings to Serve' by Janet and Geoff Benge.